improve your
opening play
CHRIS WARD

EVERYMAN CHESS

First published 2000 by Everyman Publishers plc, formerly Cadogan Books plc, Gloucester Mansions, 140A Shaftesbury Avenue, London WC2H 8HD

British Library Cataloguing-in-Publication Data
A catalogue record for this book is available from the British Library.

ISBN 1 85744 236 9

Distributed in North America by The Globe Pequot Press, 6 Business Park Road, P.O. Box 833, Old Saybrook, Connecticut 06475-0833.
Telephone 1-800-243 0495 (toll free)

All other sales enquiries should be directed to Everyman Chess, Gloucester Mansions, 140A Shaftesbury Avenue, London WC2H 8HD
tel: 0171 539 7600 fax: 0171 379 4060
email: dan@everyman.uk.com
website: www.everyman.uk.com

To my dear Grandma

EVERYMAN CHESS SERIES (formerly Cadogan Chess)
Chief Advisor: Garry Kasparov
Advisory Panel: Andrew Kinsman and Byron Jacobs

Typeset and edited by First Rank Publishing, Brighton
Production by Book Production Services
Printed and bound in Great Britain by The Cromwell Press Ltd.

Contents

Chapter One

Opening Fundamentals

- The Basic Idea of the Opening
- About this Book

The Basic Idea of the Opening

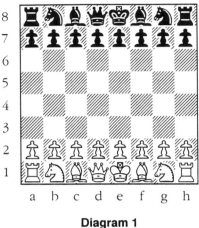

Diagram 1
Let's get ready to rumble!

Welcome to this book, in which I will be taking you through the chess openings of today and trying to explain to you why it is that theory is as it is. Throughout this book you will notice common themes regarding the explanation of most moves, and before we begin in earnest let me offer some general information regarding the early stages of a game. I know that you may have heard some of these tips before, but as far as I'm concerned, you can never be told them enough times!

 TIP: Put your pawns in the centre.

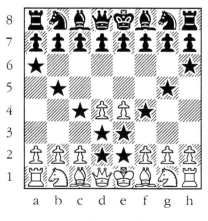

Diagram 2
The white bishops are free

If White were to have two moves at the start of the game then he could do a lot worse than to play 1 e4 and 1 d4 to seize space in the centre.

These pawns could then advance further up the board to take squares away from the opponent's pieces.

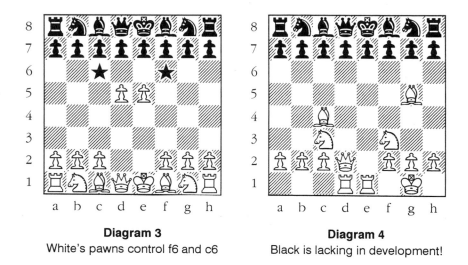

Diagram 3
White's pawns control f6 and c6

Diagram 4
Black is lacking in development!

Knights are the only pieces that can jump, so it's clear that one needs to advance a pawn or two in order to let the other pieces out. If as White you can get one pawn on e4 and one on d4, then for starters your bishops have plenty of options. Advance these centre pawns a square further up the board and the enemy knights are severely restricted (see Diagram 3).

TIP: Develop your pieces as quickly as possible.

Diagram 4 shows a model form of development for White.

Although much later in the game it may be possible to promote a pawn into a queen, it's fair to say that throughout a chess struggle, it is generally the pieces that do most of the hard work. The pieces are your core army and you must be sure to use them to maximum effect.

Whilst I will continue to stress that you shouldn't leave some of your firepower at home watching the TV, it is also clear that there is no such thing as a 'perfect' piece configuration. Where you should deploy your pieces will usually depend on where your opponent deploys his own pieces.

NOTE: In general, at least one of the knights will be developed before the bishops are brought out.

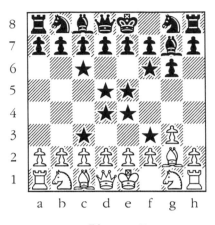

Diagram 5

The bishops pressurise the opponent's queenside

NOTE: Some like the 'Fianchetto'!

Despite my suggestion about putting pawns in the centre, many players prefer an alternative approach. Indeed one thing you will most certainly learn from this book, is that openings are a matter of taste. Although it seems like an attractive prospect to dominate the centre of the board, in fact there are many players who prefer to avoid the responsibility of having to keep everything under control, in favour of a quieter life. For Black, a fianchetto (characterised by deploying a bishop on the square directly in front of where the knight starts) is often later followed by a counter-strike in the centre. As you will see, when playing with White it is also possible to combine the two ideas.

We now start with our first exercise. (You will the answers to the exercises in Chapter Seven, but no cheating!)

Exercise 1 Does the rule of 'knights before bishops' apply with a fianchetto?

NOTE: Most strong players will try to castle early, although there will be occasions when it is satisfactory not to do so.

If you don't castle early then you must always be aware of any checks (Diagram 6).

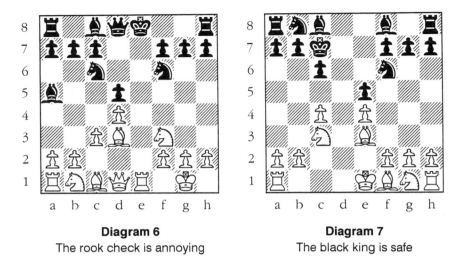

Diagram 6	Diagram 7
The rook check is annoying	The black king is safe

Sometimes, however, the king can find a safe haven without the need for castling (Diagram 7).

TIP: Plan a pawn break.

But note that this does not involve plotting to throw a pawn against the ground as hard as you can! What it actually means is that you should try to engineer a pawn move that will put pressure on your opponent's position. This may then enable you to bring your rooks into the game effectively.

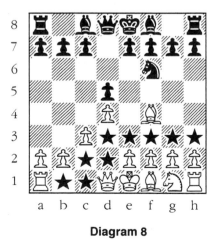

Diagram 8
Zigzagging a rook into play is impractical here

Of course rooks are valuable pieces and deserve to play an important role in the game. There can be no arguing the influence

9

they have in endings, frequently nipping around attacking pawns and such like. However, whilst it's clear that the opening is a good battleground for knights and bishops, only too often the rooks are left out in the cold for too long.

It is difficult to introduce them into the action without a pawn break first. Put simply, attempting to bring rooks out in front of your pawns is awkward and when there are so many pieces still around, they are bound to be vulnerable to enemy pieces of lesser value.

Occasionally in the middlegame, when the pawns offer some cover (e.g. with the f5 one in Diagram 9) it is possible to swing a rook or two up and along. In general though the first stage to activating a rook is to challenge an enemy pawn with one of yours. When there is no side-stepping to be done, the likely outcome will be the creation of one or two open or half-open files, as in Diagram 10.

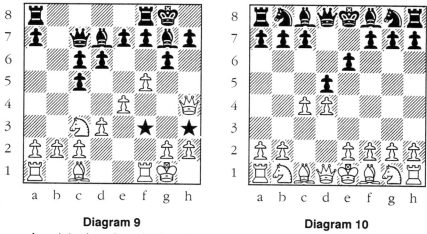

Diagram 9

A rook 'swinger' can be handy

Diagram 10

Taking on d5 opens lines for the rooks

Here the pawn break c2-c4 has set the ball rolling. Both sides must begin developing their pieces, but the future may easily hold possibilities for the rooks along the c- and e-files.

 NOTE: Although one cannot categorically state that bishops are better than knights, you will often find that other things being equal, more often than not a bishop will avoid an unprovoked swap for a knight. Obviously it depends upon the situation, but similarly a knight will frequently be happy to

concede itself for a bishop provided it isn't making a concession elsewhere.

TIP: The direction in which the fixed pawns lean gives a good indication as to which side of the board one should dedicate one's resources.

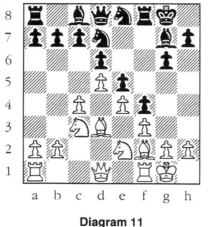

Diagram 11

Exercise 2: On which side of the board are both players likely to get most joy?

About this Book

Often when teaching juniors who have been bemused by the existence of numerous openings, I try to prevent them from being 'blinded by science'. Up to a certain point, provided that you are aware of basic principles and ideas, there is no need to start booking up on pages of theory that may take much of the fun out of the game if you attempt to learn it parrot fashion. On the other hand, I'm sure that many players believe that while it is the competing that counts, it's far more enjoyable when you win!

In this book I have tried to demonstrate that there is more to chess openings than just putting your pawns in the centre and developing your pieces (although that's not a bad place to start!). I haven't covered every single possible opening, but there is a pretty reasonable selection. Perhaps it is not important whether a variation is named after a famous player or a country's capital, but taking on board some of the features of lines that have yet to cross your path, can only help improve your understanding of the game.

It naturally follows that as you improve you will seek out far more detail and numerous variations in texts specific to your favourite opening and if it's plain moves you're after then you're better off with the *BCO's*, *ECO's* and *NCO's* of this world. My aim here is to provide the reader with an instructive introduction to a variety of ways to approach the start of a chess game.

There are dozens of openings out there, so what are we waiting for? Let's get on with it!

Summary

Put your pawns in the centre.

Develop your pieces as quickly as possible.

In general, at least one of the knights will be developed before the bishops are brought out.

Plan a pawn break.

The direction in which the fixed pawns lean gives a good indication as to which side of the board one should dedicate one's resources.

Chapter Two

Symmetrical e-pawn Openings

- ◼ Scotch Game ◼ Centre Game
- ◼ Ponziani Opening ◼ Ruy Lopez Opening
- ◼ Italian Game ◼ Two Knights Defence
- ◼ Four Knights Game
- ◼ Vienna Game ◼ King's Gambit
- ◼ Petroff Defence
- ◼ Philidor Defence

In this chapter we shall concentrate on the v openings that can arise after the moves

1 e4

Putting a pawn in the centre where it controls squares (namely d5 and f5) and immediately pr for the queen and bishop.

1...e5

A blocker! Black follows suit, thus receiving similar benefits.

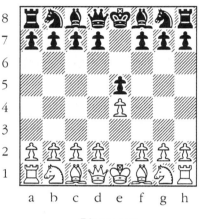

Diagram 1
Not conceding ground!

Let's start with one of the oldest openings, the Scotch Game.

Scotch Game

1 e4 e5 2 Nf3

Developing a knight and attacking Black's e5-pawn.

2...Nc6

Developing a knight and defending the e-pawn. Things are pretty straightforward so far!

3 d4

This move introduces the Scotch Opening; a good place to start because it all seems so logical. White places another pawn in the centre and, although this pawn's life expectancy isn't looking too great, already White has made his pawn break.

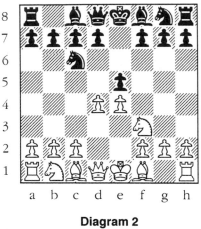

Diagram 2
Looking good

3...exd4

The only sensible response. Black's e-pawn was under attack twice and if he chose to defend it, White also has the option of advancing his d-pawn to gain more space and hassle the c6-knight.

Note that 3...Bb4+? would achieve very little for Black after 4 c3! In order to solve both the attack on the bishop and the e-pawn, Black would then have to retreat his bishop to d6. On that square it would obstruct the d7-pawn which in turn would obstruct the c8-bishop which in turn would obstruct the a8-rook. A most undesirable knock-on effect!

TIP: It is always wise to keep an eye out for checks because sometimes there might be a very good one on offer. However, that is not to say you should give one at every opportunity!

4 Nxd4

A possible alternative here for White is the rather odd-looking 4 c3 (see Diagram 3).

This move is known as the Scotch Gambit, and the idea is that after 4... dxc3 5 Nxc3, in exchange for his sacrificed pawn, White has achieved speedier development.

WARNING: Beware of accepting gambits – your opponent can get a big lead in development and this can be very dangerous.

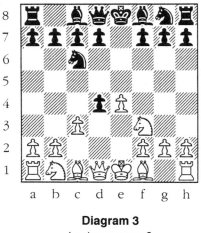

Diagram 3
Losing a pawn?

Now let's return to the position after 4 Nxd4.

4...Nf6

Sensibly developing the other knight and hitting White's e-pawn in the process.

Exercise 3 Instead would it not be wise for Black to trade knights in the centre, thus dragging the enemy queen into the middle and reaching the position below?

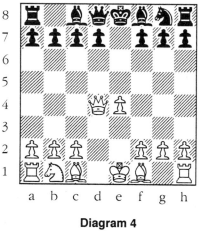

Diagram 4
A well or badly placed white queen?

So 4...Nf6 is a better move than 4...Nxd4, with the only other sensible continuation being 4...Bc5. In that event White would have to do something about his knight in the middle as it

17

would be under threat from two black pieces. Suggestions include trading knights on c6, protecting it with 5 Be3 and retreating it with 5 Nb3. Regarding the latter, it is generally not advisable to keep moving the same piece so often in the opening/middlegame, but the blow would be softened here by the fact that a tempo would be gained on Black's c5-bishop.

5 Nc3

Strictly speaking, we are now entering an opening known as the Scotch Four Knights. White has to do something about protecting his e-pawn, but must not forget that his d4-knight requires support. For example 5 Bd3?? would interrupt the queen's view, thus blundering a piece to 5...Nxd4.

The main alternative here is 5 Nxc6 bxc6 and then 6 e5 (previously unplayable because the c6-knight covered this square), putting the question to the black knight. Its safest square (where it is also of some use) is on d5, but interestingly usually Black prefers to throw in 6...Qe7 first. This pins the e-pawn to White's king, with 7 Qe2 being the only satisfactory way to protect the e5-pawn and break the pin.

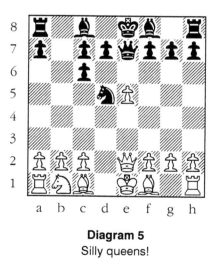

Diagram 5
Silly queens!

Frankly both queens look daft stuck in front of their kings and obstructing their own bishops, but Black's logic behind 6...Qe7 is that this trade is worse for his opponent than for himself.

5...Bb4

Developing the bishop and at the same time pinning the white knight to the king. The upshot of this is that effectively White's e4-pawn is no longer protected and rather than 6...Bxc3+ 7 bxc3 Nxe4, Black simply threatens 6...Nxe4. This may seem obvious to the reader, but it is a very important point and one so often overlooked by juniors. By preserving the bishop Black has more options.

TIP: Bishops are excellent at pinning enemy knights (to kings, queens and sometimes rooks). However, that does not necessarily mean that they are happy to exchange themselves for the trusted steeds.

6 Nxc6

Paving the way for White's next move. White does not want to bring his queen out yet with say the ugly looking 6 Qd3 and he cannot really justify a pawn move (6 f3) when there is still development to be getting on with.

TIP: When there are more important things to be doing (like completing one's development), one shouldn't fiddle around with little pawn moves.

6...bxc6

This changes Black's pawn structure significantly, but is the correct choice. To recapture the other way would allow an unfavourable trade of queens as Black would no longer be able to castle. In addition he would simply have an inferior pawn structure as there is no easy way to undouble his c-pawns.

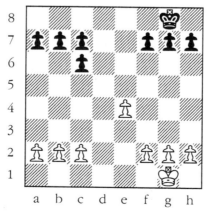

Diagram 6
Unlike his opponent, White has an 'effective' pawn majority

7 Bd3

Often it is true to say that bishops don't like just defending pawns. However, the e4-pawn is not blocked and thus there is potential for the bishop along the d3-h7 diagonal. Besides, White is ready to castle.

7...0-0 8 0-0

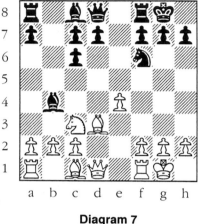

Diagram 7
Black has two half-open files

TIP: The general rule of thumb is that the fewer the pawn islands you have, the better off you are.

In diagram 7, Black has three pawn 'islands' (pawn groupings) compared to White's two. Black clearly has the inferior structure as he has an isolated a-pawn (lacking any compatriot pawns around to help it!) and doubled c-pawns. However, doubled pawns are not always a bad thing. For starters (unless you have sneaked nine pawns on to the board!) there will be at least one half-open file. Here there are two, with Black also having the potential to finish up with a useful centre pawn.

8...d5 9 exd5

A common mistake here is for White to advance his pawn with 9 e5. The e5-square is a nice one for the pawn, but after 9...Ng4 White could easily find himself in hot water. The h2- and f2-pawns are potential targets along with the e5-pawn. White is unable to defend that with 10 f4 as Black can win the exchange with 10...Bc5+ (and note this is another good reason why Black has withheld from swapping the bishop for the knight on c3, even though that would have meant messing up White's queenside pawn structure) 11 Kh1 Nf2+.

9...cxd5 10 Bg5

White's last minor piece is brought into play, pinning the knight and thus pressurising Black's d5-pawn.

10...c6

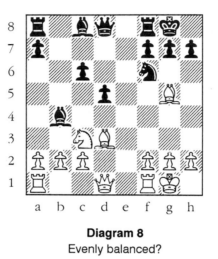

Diagram 8
Evenly balanced?

Black offers support to his d-pawn. White may want to start thinking about bringing his major pieces in on the act (e.g. Qf3 and Re1). He has a well co-ordinated position and arguably a very small advantage.

Centre Game

1 e4 e5 2 d4

Taking the concept of putting your pawns in the centre rather too literally. As in the Scotch Game, this pawn will be snatched off.

2...exd4 3 Qxd4

Personally, I don't have a great deal of respect for this opening, but as it has taken a few scalps in its time, it must be taken seriously. Compared to our little discussion about centralised queens in the last section, I would have to say that White's queen is not well placed here.

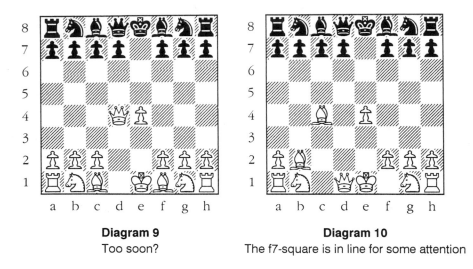

Diagram 9

Too soon?

Diagram 10

The f7-square is in line for some attention

One alternative is to go into gambit mode stakes with 3 c3 and upon 3...dxc3, how does 4 Bc4 cxb2 5 Bxb2 (Diagram 10) take your fancy?

Here we see the so-called Danish Gambit, in which White offers to sacrifice two pawns for a big lead in development. One well-known antidote is to return a pawn immediately with 5...d5 6 Bxd5 Nf6.

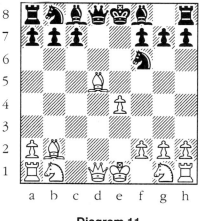

Diagram 11

Exercise 4: Does 7 Bxf7+ win the black queen?

NOTE: Gambits don't always have to be accepted and sometimes material can be effectively returned at a later date.

3...Nc6

Developing the knight with tempo as the white queen must move again.

4 Qe3

An ugly-looking place to park the queen, but the only method in White's apparent madness is that, having evacuated d1 with his queen, he is one step nearer to long castling.

5...Nf6 6 Nc3 Bb4

Black pressurises the e4-pawn by pinning one of its protectors.

7 Bd2 0-0 8 0-0-0 Re8

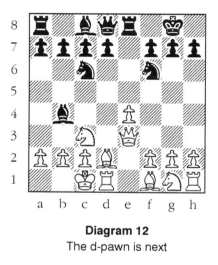

Diagram 12
The d-pawn is next

Black has held back on a routine ...d7-d6 because he harbours dreams of getting in ...d7-d5 in one go. His position here is perfectly okay.

Ponziani Opening

1 e4 e5 2 Nf3 Nc6 3 c3

Although the Ponziani Opening is rarely seen in Grandmaster chess these days, the principle of c2-c3 is used in many symmetrical e-pawn variations. Quite simply White wants to end up with a strong pawn centre and prepares d2-d4 such that ...e5xd4 can be met by c3xd4, when his aim would be achieved.

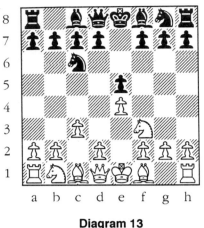

Diagram 13
The scene is set for d2-d4

It should be clear that the drawback of c2-c3 is that it deprives the queen's knight of its most natural square; a feature which Black is quick to exploit.

3...Nf6

This attacks the e-pawn, which has no obvious good volunteers for defence. The other popular response that takes advantage of White's last move is 3...d5. The point is that after 4 exd5 Qxd5, the black queen would be in a good position due to Nc3 not being on the menu.

4 d4

White must persevere as moves like 4 Qc2 or 4 d3 are too slow and do not fit in with his plan.

4...exd4

Sometimes sending a knight out on a limb can be risky, but actually here there are no real problems with the alternative 4...Nxe4 5 d5 Ne7 6 Nxe5 Ng6.

5 e5 (Diagram 14)

This theme is worth remembering. White wasn't about to celebrate getting his desired centre with 5 cxd4?, only to see one of the pawns drop with 5...Nxe4. On the face of it seems that White has gained the upper hand because after the attacked black knight moves, White will regain his pawn and have a handy pawn chain in the centre. However, both 5...Ne4 6 cxd4 d5 and 5...Nd5 6 cxd4 d6 are playable for Black. In the former case he will have a foothold in the centre and in the latter he can try to prove that White has over-extended himself by chiselling away at the centre at a later date.

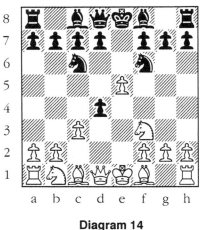

Diagram 14
A couple of gaps emerge

Ruy Lopez Opening

1 e4 e5 2 Nf3 Nc6 3 Bb5

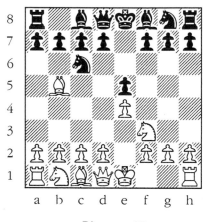

Diagram 15
The popular Ruy Lopez or Spanish Opening

The move 3 Bb5 introduces one of the most popular openings known to Grandmaster chess – the Ruy Lopez or Spanish Opening. White develops the bishop so that it pressurises the black knight, which is currently guarding the e5-pawn, and at the same time prepares to castle kingside.

TIP: When stuck between deciding on which piece to develop, give preference to one on the side that you expect to castle.

It should be noted that in fact White is not actually threatening to win a pawn with 4 Bxc6 followed by 5 Nxe5. This explains why the most popular continuation for Black is

3...a6

If White now decides to enter a bishop for knight trade, then he is selecting the Exchange Variation. The key point though is that after 4 Bxc6 dxc6, Black can meet 5 Nxe5? with 5...Qd4, forking both e4 and e5, and thus guaranteeing the material is returned. Note that this wouldn't be the case were White already castled as then White would have a pin on the open e-file, as in Diagram 16.

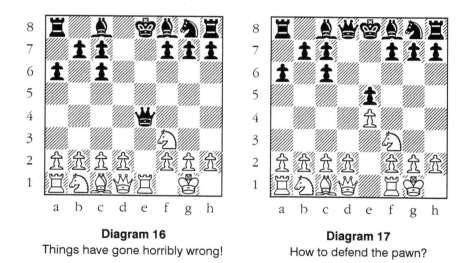

Diagram 16	Diagram 17
Things have gone horribly wrong!	How to defend the pawn?

Okay so Black lost a move somewhere in Diagram 16, but it's clear that 5 0-0 (after 4 Bxc6 dxc6) now threatens to win the pawn (Diagram 17) and Black must do something about it.

WARNING: Beware placing your king in front of your king on an open file!

Well, 5...f6 would normally be an ugly move as it exposes the b3-g8 diagonal. However. White's light-squared bishop is no longer on the board, and since that would have been the piece to prevent Black from castling, it is acceptable to play 5...f6 here, even though the black knight must find somewhere else (e7 being a prime candidate) to go.

Alternatively Black could defend the e5-pawn with a bishop, either directly with 5...Bd6 or indirectly with the pin on the knight by 5...Bg4.

4 Ba4

Although the Exchange Variation is a safe way for White to play for a slight edge, most top players prefer to preserve the bishop, simply retreating it to a4.

4...Nf6 5 0-0

Diagram 18
Ignoring the attack on the e4-pawn

And now we are slowly getting into the nitty-gritty of one of the toughest openings to handle. If you can get to grips with this one, then the rest will seem like a walk in the park!

Here Black can choose to enter the Open Variation by capturing White's e-pawn. However, although on 5...Nxe4 White can regain the pawn instantly with 6 Re1, in fact 6 d4!? is more challenging as Black must be careful not to end up losing his knight by getting it pinned to his king. Instead

5...Be7

is more cautious as it offers cover to the king and prepares kingside castling.

6 Re1

Finally defending the e-pawn. At first it may seem as though an important piece, the rook, has been assigned a menial task. The point though is that White doesn't want to put the knight on c3 because that's where he intends placing a pawn and although 6 d3 is eminently playable, White is also hoping to occupy the centre with d2-d4 in one turn.

6...b5

In all probability it has no doubt crossed your mind whether Black should be doing this, and if so, why was White encouraging it? Well, although this advance kind of gains space for Black, in general White is hoping that such an expansion will prove to be a weakness. However, it was no longer satisfactory for Black to just continue with his development. White was threatening to win a pawn with 7 Bxc6 dxc6 8 Nxe5 as here White's own e-pawn was adequately protected.

 WARNING: General principles and such like are all very well, but one must always pay attention to day-to-day matters.

7 Bb3 0-0 8 c3

A characteristic move of the Ruy Lopez. Not for the first time we see White eager to build a strong pawn centre with d2-d4. As it happens though this allows Black to if so desired select the highly contentious Marshall Gambit with 8...d5 9 exd5 Nxd5 10 Nxe5 Nxe5 11 Rxe5 c6 12 d4 Bd6 13 Re1 Qh4.

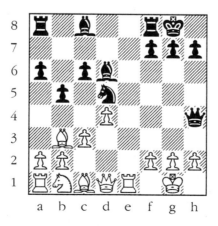

Diagram 19
The Marshall Gambit – Black is on the offensive

After 14 g3, White is a pawn up, but he must deal with a lot of enemy activity. As defending in this manner is not everybody's cup of tea, there are various Anti-Marshall Systems available to White. These include immediate logical pawn breaks 8 a4 and 8 d4 as well as the quiet 8 d3 (which certainly doesn't rule out a later plan of c2-c3 and d2-d4).

8...d6

Black may also interchange this with 7...0-0 as he too might not desire the complications of the Marshall Gambit.

9 h3

Cautiously eliminating a future ...Bg4 from Black's options; a possibility that could easily place White's central dominance plans at risk.

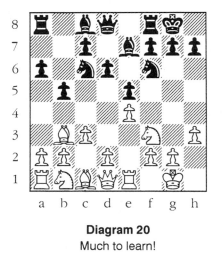

Diagram 20
Much to learn!

Many variations spring from the above position, although there are several underlying themes. Whilst White will get in his d2-d4 push, Black would rather bolster his e5-pawn (e.g. with ...Re8 and ...Bf8) than effectively trade it for White's c3-pawn. White will usually opt to keep his light-squared bishop out of the evil clutches of Black's knights and his own queenside knight often embarks on a Nbd2-f1-g3 journey.

NOTE: You may occasionally see strong players retreat their bishops to base, having first brought out their rooks. As bishops are long-range pieces, they can of course rest on one side of the board and still have an influence on the other.

Italian Game

1 e4 e5 2 Nf3 Nc6 3 Bc4

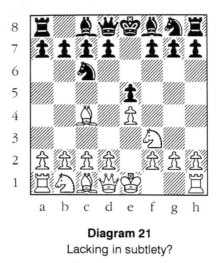

Diagram 21
Lacking in subtlety?

Here we turn to the beginner's favourite, known as the Italian Game or Giuoco Piano. White gets straight to the point by deploying his bishop on an active diagonal where it homes in on the traditional weak point, f7. Here the bishop doesn't travel 'all round the houses' via b5, a4 and b3 to get to this diagonal as in the Ruy Lopez, but you will no doubt later see some similarities.

3...Bc5

Although I'm certainly not saying that this piece deployment should be ruled out in the Spanish, Black is not feeling the strain of his e5-pawn quite so much here, and is perhaps entitled to be a touch more ambitious with his bishop. The other sensible continuation 3...Nf6 is covered in the next section.

Exercise 5: After the more passive 3...Be7 4 d4 exd4 5 c3 dxc3 6 Qd5 leading to Diagram 22, might Black just as well resign?

4 c3

Again we see this move, with the prospect of d2-d4 looking even more tempting in view of the fact that it would attack the enemy bishop. So a pawn break is planned, but is there anything wrong with simple development? Well let's just play some simple moves, say 4 Nc3 d6 5 d3 Nf6 (Diagram 23).

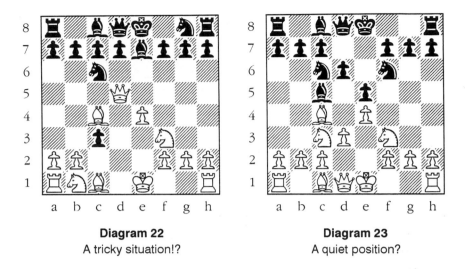

Diagram 22
A tricky situation!?

Diagram 23
A quiet position?

Now it would be negligent of me not to mention a popular trick amongst juniors, which is to pin the f6-knight with 6 Bg5 and in the event of say 6...0-0?, follow it up with 7 Nd5. The wrecking of Black's kingside pawn structure around his king is potentially fatal and both 8 Bxf6 gxf6 9 Qd2 (planning Qh6) and 8 Nxf6+ gxf6 9 Bh6 are extremely dangerous continuations for Black.

Here Black was naive in just castling and the danger could have been avoided with 6...h6 7 Bh4 g5. Then after 8 Bg3, it would be White's turn to deal with the pin after 8...Bg4. It is not a disaster for Black to advance his h- and g-pawns in this manner as he has not yet castled on that side and could instead consider long castling at a later stage.

Clearly then it is not necessary to prevent the pin altogether, although again I have noticed that an obsession with this theme often leads youngsters to take time out to prevent the pin with the moves h2-h3 and ...h7-h6.

Exercise 6: (Diagram 24) What have both sides forgotten about?

Finally a quick word on 4 b4, the Evans Gambit. If the gambit is accepted, this allows White to get in c2-c3 with tempo and hence d2-d4 quickly too.

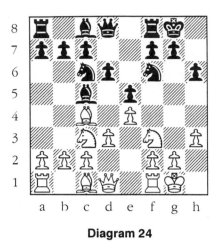

Diagram 24

 NOTE: Gambits are difficult things to access. All I can say is that they are rarely permanent fixtures in repertoires of top players, particularly in these days of materialistic computer-aided analysis.

4...Nf6 5 d4

The most aggressive response, although not necessarily the best one. A quieter approach is 5 d3. This protects the e4-pawn and although it puts d2-d4 on hold for the time being, White certainly wouldn't rule out this central push once he has completed his development. After say 5...d6 6 0-0 0-0

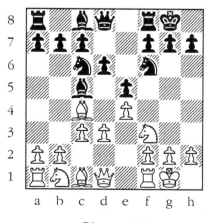

Diagram 25
The squares b4 and d4 are under control

there are several ideas available to him. He may care to develop his queen's knight on the kingside (via d2 and f1) as in the Ruy Lopez and as well as the obvious d3-d4 pawn break, he may consider expanding on the queenside with moves like b2-b4 and a2-a4. For Black's part, he may consider preparing his own pawn break with ...d6-d5 or ...f7-f5.

5...exd4 6 cxd4

White has bought some time for his attacked e-pawn because Black is now obliged to move his bishop. After the main alternative 6 e5, a critical concept comes to light.

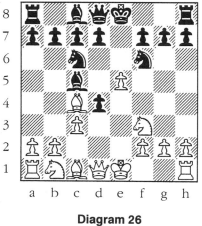

Diagram 26
The standard treatment is 6...d5!

Black cannot afford to grovel around the edges as after say 6...Ng4? 7 cxd4, his pieces will be uncoordinated with White having a stronghold in the centre. Instead he must reply with 6...d5!, temporarily ignoring the attack on his knight in favour of hitting the enemy bishop. Should White capture this pawn en passant then Black will have no worries. After 7 Bb5, he has a nice home for his knight on e4, whilst the complications of 7 exf6 dxc4 8 fxg7 Rg8 are fine for Black because of his lead in development and fantastic bishop pair.

TIP: In Open Games, even if he chooses to reject the notion, Black should always consider meeting e4-e5 with ...d7-d5.

6...Bb4+

Not giving White time to consolidate his attractive pawn centre.

7 Bd2

7 Nc3 looks natural until we notice that this knight is pinned and thus not protecting the e-pawn. Nevertheless, this is a popular variation at club level with White offering more wood for the fire after 7...Nxe4 8 0-0. Note that it certainly is possible for Black to be too greedy, e.g. 8...Nxc3 9 bxc3 Bxc3 10 Qb3 Bxa1 11 Bxf7+ Kf8 12 Bg5 Ne7 13 Ne5 Bxd4 14 Bg6 (threatening Qf7 mate) 14...d5 15 Qf3+ Bf5 16 Bxf5 Bxe5 17 Be6+ Bf6 18 Bxf6 gxf6 19 Qxf6+ Ke8 20 Qf7 mate! (Diagram 27)

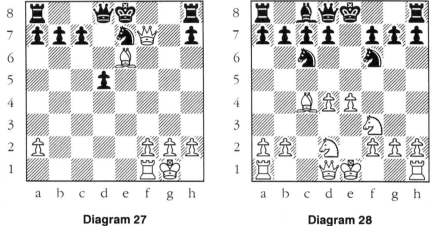

Diagram 27
Not a bad opening!

Diagram 28
A fast reaction is required

 WARNING: Beware grabbing too much material. Of course we all like to take our opponent's pieces, but you only really need so much extra material to guarantee victory.

Instead a safer continuation is 8...Bxc3 when if White simply recaptures (9 bxc3) then Black can get in 9...d5 with the comfort of 10...0-0 to follow next.

7...Bxd2+ 8 Nbxd2 (Diagram 28)

White seems to have it made and Black's next move is critical.

9...d5!

Breaking up the White central pawn duo.

10 exd5 Nxd5

White has a lead in development, but he also has an isolated pawn which is well blockaded.

Two Knights Defence

1 e4 e5 2 Nf3 Nc6 3 Bc4 Nf6

Diagram 29
Knights before bishops!

Black has developed very naturally and with his logical last move some fascinating complications are encouraged. Black is attacking the e4-pawn, and something worth observing is that here 4 Nc3 (as we have seen before, not really much help on the rook activation front) can be met by a basic tactic 4...Nxe4. The simple idea is that should White just take the knight (5 Nxe4) then the fork 5...d5 guarantees a return. Note here an advanced concept which is that after 6 Bb5 dxe4 7 Nxe5, the crafty 7...Qg5 comes into play. On g5 the queen attacks the knight and through to the bishop as well as the g2-pawn. This is a better method of dealing with the c6-pin than say 7...Bd7.

Exercise 7 If after 4...Nxe4, White acknowledges that he will lose the piece back anyway, is it worth him flicking in 5 Bxf7+ Kxf7 6 Nxe4, to reach the position in Diagram 30?

4 Ng5

Wow, radical!

NOTE: Most players adhere to the principle that you shouldn't move one piece twice before moving others once.

The above suggestion breaks that rule, but certainly tests Black's mettle. A similar theme to one we have seen before arises after another club player's favourite: 4 d4 exd4, the Max Lange Attack. Now on 5 0-0 Bc5 6 e5 or the immediate 5 e5, arguably Black's best reply is ...d7-d5 (Diagram 31).

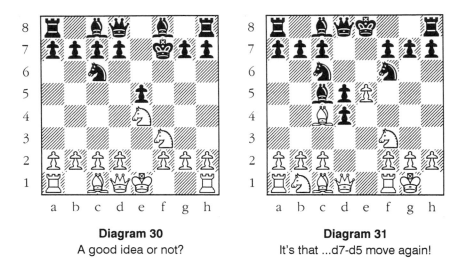

Diagram 30
A good idea or not?

Diagram 31
It's that ...d7-d5 move again!

As we saw in the previous section, 4 d3 would be a quieter approach, but nevertheless this is still employed by strong players who intend the flexible (in terms of pawn breaks and general expansion) c2-c3 rather than Nc3.

After 4 Ng5 it certainly pays for Black to be aware of some opening theory in this sharp position.

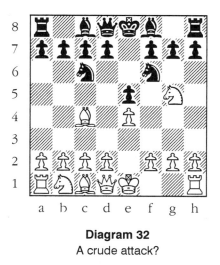

Diagram 32
A crude attack?

Exercise 8: As Black, how would you deal with the threat on f7?

4...d5 5 exd5

Now follows possibly the greatest surprise of all and frankly it's very difficult to explain in terms of opening principles.

Black should not continue with the obvious 5...Nxd5? as the latent pressure on f7 is too strong. In fact 6 d4! exd4 (6...Nxd4 loses a piece after 7 c3) 7 0-0 Be7 is losing to 8 Nxf7! Kxf7 9 Qh5+. An attempt to protect the twice-attacked knight with 9...Ke6 falls flat on account of 10 Re1+. Worth mentioning too is 7...Be6 8 Re1 Qd7 when White can deliver a crushing blow.

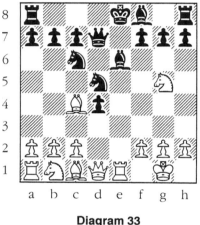

Diagram 33
Prepare yourself for a stunner!

Did you spot 9 Nxf7!! Well, then you would have observed that 9...Bxf7 is illegal, 9...Qxf7 leaves the d5-knight en prise and 9...Kxf7 10 Qf3+ is devastating because of either 10...Kg8 11 Rxe6 Qxe6 12 Bxd5 or 10...Kg6 11 Rxe6+ Qxe6 12 Bd3+.

5...Na5

Instead opening theory tells us that Black needs to take steps to remove White's bishop from its current menacing diagonal. Notoriously, this method of defence involves sacrificing a pawn and the same can be said of another bizarre approach, 5...b5, which is also blatantly designed to lure the bishop away.

TIP: Generally knights on the rim are considered dim. However, although it's true that they have less options there, placing one on the edge is of course acceptable if there is a good reason for it.

6 Bb5+

Retreating the bishop elsewhere would just enable Black to safely recapture the d-pawn. Now it is possible for Black to simply block the check with his bishop, but that leaves his a5-knight out in the cold. Instead this whole line hinges on the following continuation:

6...c6 7 dxc6 bxc6

Black leaves both the a- and c-pawns isolated, but forces the bishop to move yet again.

8 Be2

The poor co-ordination of White's pieces is well illustrated after 8 Ba4?! h6 9 Nf3 e4 10 Ne5 Qd4!, when the knight and bishop are forked and 11 Bxc6+ Nxc6 12 Nxc6 Qc5 leaves the knight doomed.

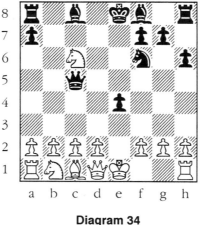

Diagram 34
Stranded!

> **NOTE: Knights tend to dislike open spaces, generally preferring to have pawns around to look after them. A knight stuck out on its own can be a liability rather than a strength.**

8...h6

Now Black uses the offside nature of the white knight to his advantage by incorporating useful moves whilst attacking it.

9 Nf3 e4 10 Ne5 Bd6

Black has good development in exchange for the pawn.

Four Knights Game

1 e4 e5 2 Nf3 Nc6 3 Nc3 Nf6

Well, all four knights are out and you have probably guessed how this opening earned its name!

Diagram 35
Knights before bishops!

It is worth noting that in the event of 3...Bc5 instead of 3..Nf6, White has the 4 Nxe5 Nxe5 5 d4 fork trick available to him. We saw this theme in the Italian Game and it occasionally appears in this opening too.

4 Bb5

4 d4 would transpose to the Scotch Four Knights, which we saw earlier in this book. With the text White is threatening the e5-pawn after chopping off its defender on c6 (note that unlike in the Ruy Lopez, Black wouldn't be able to win it back with ...Qd4).

It seems that symmetry is definitely the name of the game here and if Black doesn't want to delve into the complications of 4...Bc5 5 Nxe5 (before or after both sides castle) or 4...Nd4, then it seems he should follow suit with 4...Bb4. Then 5 0-0 0-0 6 d3 d6 may follow and no doubt this very basic chess may appeal to many beginners. Again though I would stress my concern about the lack of thought given to how the rooks may emerge.

Vienna Game

1 e4 e5 2 Nc3

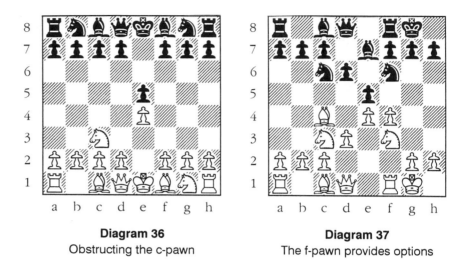

Diagram 36
Obstructing the c-pawn

Diagram 37
The f-pawn provides options

I quite like the general idea behind this opening. White ignores a usual c2-c3 plan and in fact aims for the alternative pawn break to d2-d4, namely f2-f4. Indeed if Black plays too passively soon everything could look very nice for White, with a position like that in Diagram 37.

Here White has several nice possibilities. At any time he could trade pawns on e5 and give himself a half-open f-file, but perhaps even more attractive would be a cramping plan spearheaded by f4-f5. Although then strictly only the e4-pawn is fixed, the natural lean of the pawns would nevertheless be toward the kingside and an attacking g4-g5 strategy would be most uncomfortable for Black.

TIP: An attack with the f-pawn can often expose your own king. However, don't rule it out as a useful commodity as in particular it can provide a required pawn break.

2...Nf6 3 Bc4

The Vienna Gambit arises if White plays the immediate 3 f4. Black is then advised not to react defensively with 3...d6, but rather with the central counter-thrust 3...d5.

TIP: Although of course the specifics of a position must be taken into account, modern chess theory nevertheless tells us that the best way to meet wing play is with action in the centre.

3...Nc6

Exercise 9 Fair enough, but hold your horses, can't Black engage that nifty 3...Nxe4 trick here, as in Diagram 38?

Diagram 38
Will this work?

4 d3 Bb4

The most active post for the bishop. The time would be right now for 5 f4, except that Black is ready for the best response 5...d5. In fact this move is what Black should be looking to play anyhow. For example, it's also sensible against 5 Nge2, but of course not on 5 Bg5 when White effectively has more control over that key central square.

King's Gambit

1 e4 e5 2 f4

This is rather more radical than its queen's pawn counterpart (1 d4 d5 2 c4), as White immediately gets in a pawn break. The King's Gambit is one of the most dangerous openings around, but it should be noted first that the h4-e1 diagonal has been opened. Hence for example if now 2...Bc5, 3 fxe5 is not advisable in view of the crushing riposte 3...Qh4+ 4 g3 Qxe4+. Hence

Nf3 is high on White's agenda.

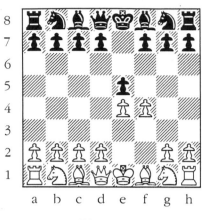

Diagram 39
White exposes his own king

2...exf4

Accepting the gambit. An active way to decline White's pawn offer is with 2...d5, which has close similarities to the Vienna Gambit.

3 Nf3

Preventing the check on h4, although I guess it's just worth mentioning that the Bishop's Gambit 3 Bc4 instead offers the f1-square to the white king, hoping that his king being inconvenienced by 3...Qh4+ will be offset by tempo gained by attacking the enemy queen (i.e. after a future Nf3 the black queen will have to move again).

3...d6

Freeing the c8-bishop, but many players prefer to leave this move for a while, instead favouring the immediate 3...g5.

4 d4

The point behind the gambit. By luring away Black's e5-pawn, White has left the way free for his pawns to dominate the centre. If White's dark-squared bishop could now take on f4 and he could develop his other bishop and castle, life could hardly be sweeter. Naturally though Black is out to spoil the party!

4...g5

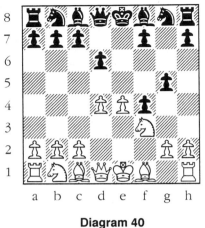

Diagram 40
Yes, that's a black pawn on f4!

And in contrast with general opening principles, we've seen too many pawn moves. However, this is hardly a regular opening. White is a pawn down (that's why it was a gambit!) and the f4-pawn is a bit of a thorn in his position. Nevertheless, White does have a lead in development, though he must usually be prepared to throw further wood on the fire if he is to obtain an attack. From Diagram 40 White can try 5 Bc4 and 6 0-0 or he may attempt to undermine Black's protection of f4 with h2-h4.

Petroff Defence

1 e4 e5 2 Nf3 Nf6

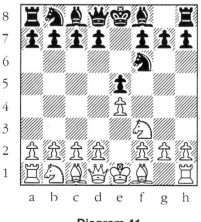

Diagram 41
A solid defence!

The Petroff Defence is often regarded as being marginally less entertaining than watching paint dry(!). Black ignores the attack on his own e-pawn in favour of hitting White's own e-pawn. A transposition into the Four Knights Game is not unlikely after 3 Nc3, but White won't want to be railroaded into that if say his main choice is the Ruy Lopez.

Here 3 d4 attempts to confuse the issue, but the most popular continuation is still:

3 Nxe5 d6

An incredibly common miniature in junior chess is 3...Nxe4? 4 Qe2 Nf6 5 Nc6+, when it's goodbye to the black queen. It might not surprise you then that Black is eager to avoid that particular continuation and opts to budge the white knight before regaining the pawn.

4 Nf3 Nxe4

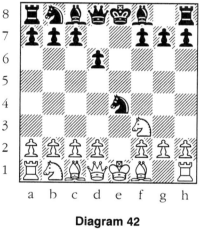

Diagram 42
How about 5 Qe2?

Exercise 10: Is 5 Qe2 a good idea here?

5 d4

Instead of forcing Black's knight away, White hopes to prove it to be out of position by attacking it later. His bishop will develop on d3 and should Black support the knight with the advance ...d7-d5, then White may later try and undermine that too with c2-c4.

Philidor Defence

1 e4 e5 2 Nf3 d6

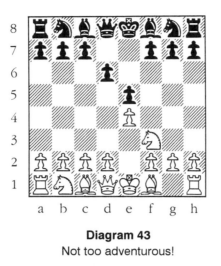

Diagram 43
Not too adventurous!

This looks slightly illogical. Black defends his e-pawn by blocking in his dark-squared bishop. It's not so bad if we remember that in several 1 e4 e5 lines, this bishop isn't necessarily destined for c5 or b4 anyway and happily rests on e7.

3 d4

This is straightforward enough though. White gets to grips with his space advantage and makes that immediate pawn break. 3 Nc3 and 3 Bc4 are of course sensible too, but 3 c3 (with d2-d4 in mind) is hardly required here.

3...Nf6

Some players prefer to trade on d4, but it certainly gives White an undisputed edge.

4 Nc3

I'm not going to dwell on the implications of 4 dxe5 here, partly because in reality these days this opening is usually reached through the move order 1 e4 d6 2 d4 Nf6 3 Nc3 e5 4 Nf3.

 WARNING: Beware transpositions from one opening to another. Even if you think you know your own openings, occasionally you can be tricked into your opponent's pet line.

4...Nbd7

A distinguishing characteristic of the Philidor. Black leaves the c6-square available for his pawn so as to be able to later claim some control over the d5-square and give his queen some freedom on c7. He temporarily blocks in his other bishop, but fulfils the role of bolstering the e5-pawn.

5 Bc4 Be7 6 0-0 0-0

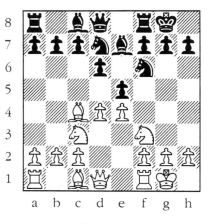

Diagram 44
Black has just enough room

There is no doubt that White has more space in which to manoeuvre his pieces, but practical play has demonstrated Black's position to be surprisingly robust.

TIP: A space advantage allows better communication of one's pieces between the kingside and the queenside. When they are cramped, it's more difficult for them to travel from one side of the board to the other.

Summary

Bishops are excellent at pinning enemy knights (to kings, queens and sometimes rooks). However, that does not necessarily mean that they are happy to exchange themselves for the trusted steeds.

When there are more important things to be doing (like completing one's development), one shouldn't fiddle around with little pawn moves.

The general rule of thumb is that the fewer the pawn islands you have, the better off you are.

Although of course the specifics of a position must be taken into account, modern chess theory nevertheless tells us that the best way to meet wing play is with action in the centre.

Chapter Three

Other Defences to 1 e4

-  Sicilian Defence ■ French Defence
- ■ Caro-Kann Defence ■ Centre Counter
- ■ Panov-Botvinnik Attack
- ■ Alekhine Defence
- ■ Pirc Defence
- ■ Nimzowitsch Defence

Sicilian Defence

1 e4 c5

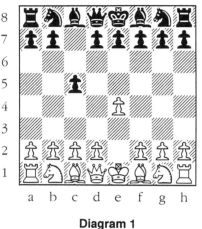

Diagram 1
The Sicilian – popular with Grandmasters

The Sicilian Defence is arguably the most exciting and aggressive defence to 1 e4, and involves Black placing a pawn where it controls an important central square. Specifically of course he is preventing White from achieving his aim of getting two pawns in the middle and, although queen development is far from a priority right now, certainly the black queen does have a way into the game for later.

There are numerous lines and variations in the Sicilian which are documented in reams of complicated theory. To give you an overview of the situation, I thought I would cover three completely different White approaches.

2 c3 Sicilian

1 e4 c5 2 c3 (Diagram 2)

No prizes for guessing that move!

White's intention is clear. He is determined to get his favourite pawn centre and, as we saw in certain 1 e4 e5 lines, he is prepared to deprive his queen's knight of its natural developing square. Black must now act quickly to prevent his opponent from reaching his goal and so for example 2...Nc6 is not the solution. Black would then only have two pieces on d4 and as

White has two covering it himself, he can just proceed with his plan (3 d4). Instead Black must target White's e-pawn, taking advantage of the fact that Nc3 is not possible.

2...d5

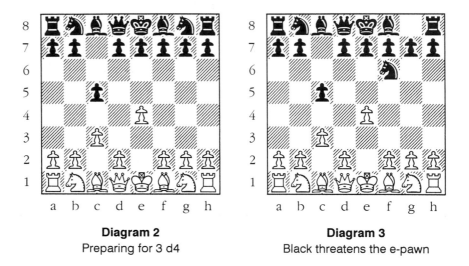

<table>
<tr><td align="center">**Diagram 2**
Preparing for 3 d4</td><td align="center">**Diagram 3**
Black threatens the e-pawn</td></tr>
</table>

Exercise 11: I consider the main alternative here to be 2...Nf6 (Diagram 3). In that event, how should White deal with the problem of his attacked e-pawn?

3 exd5

The possibility of advancing this pawn loses all of its appeal when, as is the case here, Black's light-squared bishop has not been blocked in by a pawn on e6. Here Black could develop it first, to f5 for example, before playing ...e7-e6 (compared to the next section, you will notice that this enables Black to achieve a very favourable French Defence set-up).

3...Qxd5 4 d4

Here White has established one pawn in the centre and, although the black queen is occupying an active post, there is an interesting paradox at work. In order for Black to leave White's centre weak, he will ultimately have to trade pawns on d4. That will isolate the d-pawn, but then also give his opponent back use of the c3-square. Naturally the white knight would welcome that, after which the black queen would be forced to expend another tempo moving again.

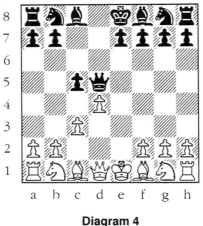

Diagram 4
The black queen is safe

Open Sicilian

1 e4 c5 2 Nf3 d6

There are many different Open Sicilians variations (with all sorts of fancy names!), and it follows that 2...e6, 2...Nc6 and 2...g6 are all reasonable alternatives depending upon the individual's taste.

3 d4

This is the pawn break that characterises the Open Sicilian. White knows that this pawn will not stay long on d4, but rather is opening lines for his pieces and allowing a knight to take centre stage.

3...cxd4 4 Nxd4 Nf6 5 Nc3

Here I would like to stop and provide you with a good cross section of the type of positions that frequently arrive in the diverse world of the Open Sicilian. Probably the only consistent element throughout is that White has a space advantage and a half-open d-file whilst Black has the corresponding half-open c-file and an extra centre pawn.

The sharp Dragon Variation arises from the moves 5...g6 6 Be3 Bg7 7 f3 0-0 8 Qd2 Nc6 9 0-0-0 (Diagram 5)

Instead of a kingside fianchetto Black can also develop flexibly with 5...a6, e.g. 6 Be2 e5 7 Nb3 Be7 8 0-0 0-0 9 Be3 Be6 10 Qd2

Nbd7, reaching the position in Diagram 6.

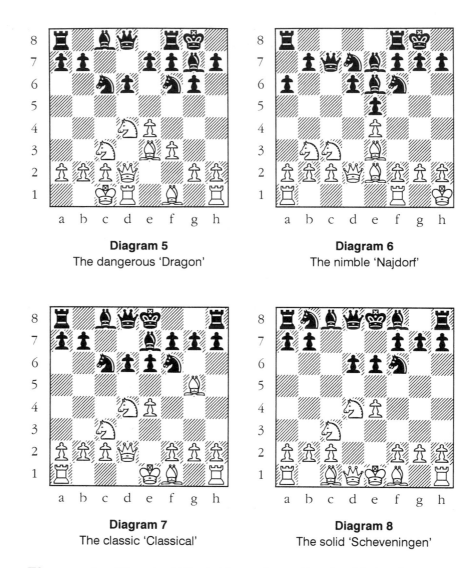

Diagram 5
The dangerous 'Dragon'

Diagram 6
The nimble 'Najdorf'

Diagram 7
The classic 'Classical'

Diagram 8
The solid 'Scheveningen'

The popular Classical Variation arises after 5...Nc6, when one common way for White to play is 6 Bg5 e6 7 Qd2 Be7, as in Diagram 7. Some grandmasters prefer the solid 5...e6 variation, reserving their options (see Diagram 8).

The Pelikan (or Sveshnikov) Variation is seen after 2...Nc6 (instead of 2...d6) 3 d4 cxd4 4 Nxd4 Nf6 5 Nc3 e5 (see Diagram 9).

The highly flexible Kan Variation arises after 2...e6 (instead of 2...d6) 3 d4 cxd4 4 Nxd4 a6, e.g. 5 Bd3 Nf6 6 0-0 Qc7 7 Qe2, as in Diagram 10.

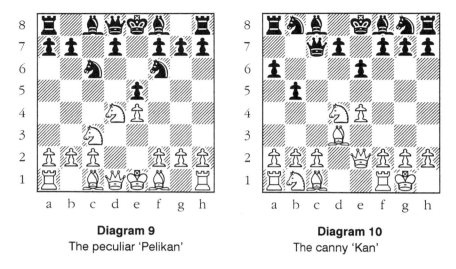

Diagram 9
The peculiar 'Pelikan'

Diagram 10
The canny 'Kan'

Grand Prix Attack and Closed Sicilian

1 e4 c5 2 Nc3 Nc6 3 f4

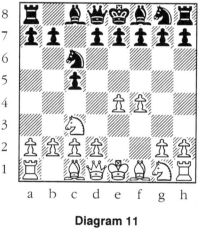

Diagram 11
Eating up space

In the so-called Grand Prix Attack, White dispenses with the general idea of the pawn break d2-d4, although he doesn't entirely rule it out as a future possibility. Instead he turns to his f-pawn to provide that bit of flexibility that is required to both aid in central control and possibly use as a springboard for an attack against the enemy king. The alternative here is the Closed Sicilian with 3 g3, whereby White engages in a quiet kingside fianchetto, but nevertheless often calls his f-pawn into active duty later anyhow.

3...g6

Although Black sometimes fianchettoes in the Open Sicilian, using the Dragon Variation, in the more closed positions a kingside fianchetto is universally accepted as a good idea. The bishop creates extra pressure in the centre, hoping to make White regret not getting in d2-d4 when he had the chance.

4 Nf3 Bg7 5 Bc4

Clearly this piece wanted to come out next in order to facilitate speedy castling. Although it doesn't actually do any pinning, 5 Bb5 would be a reasonable alternative.

5...e6

A sensible continuation that makes White's previously danger-ous looking light-squared bishop bite on granite. It also enables an alternative developing of his king's knight that is highly recommended in these variations.

6 d3 Nge7 7 0-0

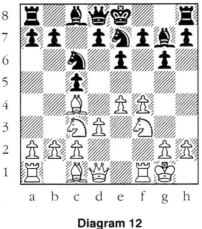

Diagram 12
Play without a pawn break

The black knight is on a far better track on e7 than it would have been on f6. Other than the obvious fact that it doesn't ob-struct the bishop, it also controls some vital squares. First, it supports a ...d7-d5 pawn push in order to regain space and embarrass the white bishop. At the same time it slows down White's desired f4-f5, a pawn push that would allow White's pieces to get at the black king. On top of that, the e7-knight could always replace the c6-knight, should that one move into the handy d4-square. Black's d6-square is weak, so he will want to avoid White from getting a half-open d-file with d3-d4. Logically the aforementioned ...Nd4 is a sure way to guarantee that d3-d4 never comes.

French Defence

1 e4 e6

On the face of it not perhaps the most impressive looking of moves. Why move a pawn one square when you can move it two?

2 d4 d5

This is the point. Giving no more ground, Black immediately strikes back in the centre. It goes without saying that a d-pawn is naturally better defended than an e-pawn because that's the file where the queens start.

Diagram 13
The e4-pawn is challenged

Now White is posed a question. What is he to do about the tension in the centre? One obvious solution is simply to trade pawns. Known as the Exchange Variation, the continuation 3 exd5 exd5 leaves the position completely symmetrical. As White would be on the move then I suppose he would have a slight initiative, but as the d5-pawn will always be well supported, Black would hardly be quaking in his boots.

TIP: When deciding whether to trade pawns, remember that effectively you will be swapping your pawn doing the initial taking with the enemy one doing the *replacing*. Above e4 for d5 seems like a fair swap, but in reality it is e4 for e6.

There are three common French Defence variations revolving around dealing with the threat to the e-pawn:

Advance Variation

1 e4 e6 2 d4 d5 3 e5

This is a very popular choice amongst juniors, whose naturally inclination when faced with a pawn challenge is to push on. Black's light-squared bishop is now rather blocked in.

NOTE: A 'bad' bishop is one whose vision is severely restricted by its own fixed pawns.

3...c5

This is a very important concept to come to grips with. Simply developing pieces will leave Black horribly cramped, whereas this simple pawn break provides him with some useful space on the queenside and something to attack (White's centre).

4 c3

Consolidating the pawn chain. If the d4-pawn is swapped off, the e5-pawn would then begin to get a little nervous.

4...Nc6 5 Nf3

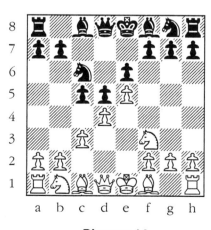

Diagram 14
The centre is blocked

Exercise 12: Any suggestions for how Black might care to continue here?

TIP: When the centre is blocked, there isn't quite the same urgency to castle.

Winawer Variation

1 e4 e6 2 d4 d5 3 Nc3

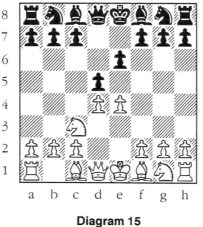

Diagram 15
Knight to the rescue

This sensible-looking move sees the knight protect the e-pawn and if Black chooses to swap on e4 now then this knight can occupy a nice central square. In that case there can be little disputing that White's space advantage leaves him with the more comfortable position.

3...Bb4

More in the spirit is for Black to continue his assault on the centre by pinning the white knight and thus once again effectively putting the question to the e4-pawn. That said, 3...Nf6 is also perfectly reasonable.

5 e5 c5

This bears a strong similarity to the Advance Variation, with Black remaining keen to undermine White's pawn centre. Obviously there is no support with c2-c3 available to White this time, but there is a continuation that achieves a similar result.

5 a3 Bxc3+ 6 bxc3

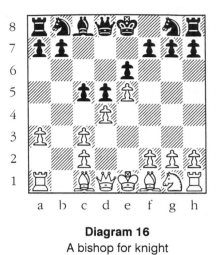

Diagram 16
A bishop for knight

We have now reached one of the most double-edged positions in modern opening theory. White has retained his strong pawn centre but picked up one or two chinks in its armour. Black's structure remains solid, but he must play out the rest of the game without his good bishop.

Tarrasch Variation

1 e4 e6 2 d4 d5 3 Nd2

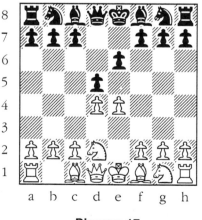

Diagram 17
The crafty pin-avoider 3 Nd2

On d2, the knight fulfils the same role as a knight on c3 (namely defending the e4-pawn), but by not obstructing the c-pawn he ensures that a ...Bb4 pin would be futile due to c2-c3. The drawback is that the knight does get in the way of the bishop on c1, although this may only be a temporary problem.

One way in which Black players often try to exploit 3 Nd2 is with 3...c5. This attacks White's currently under-defended centre and when he trades on d5, Black will have two options. He can either recapture with the pawn and argue that even if White makes it isolated (by later taking on c5), his d5-pawn won't be in line for too much attention since White's queen's knight is unable to make it to c3. Secondly, he could just meet an e4xd5 with ...Qxd5 avoiding incurring any isolated pawns. He will still have to solve the problem of activating his c8-bishop, but his queen isn't so vulnerable with Nc3 unavailable.

3...Nf6 4 e5 Nfd7

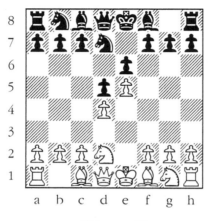

Diagram 18
The characteristic French Defence pawn structure

Again a kind of Advanced Variation has arisen, but with knights on slightly odd squares. Typical play from here on in is for Black to strike out at White's centre with ...c7-c5 and later even ...f7-f6. White usually relies on c2-c3 and has the option of f2-f4. The best square for his bishop is d3, although instead of the obvious Ngf3, he may want to try Nge2 and Ndf3 in order to provide further support to his d-pawn.

Caro-Kann Defence

1 e4 c6

Again I'd have to say why stop here rather than go on to c5? The black queen does not yet need an outlet into the game and the queen's knight is deprived of its most natural developing square.

2 d4 d5

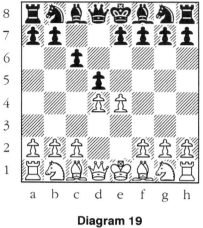

Diagram 19
The c8-bishop has a clear view

Yes, not surprisingly it was 2...d5 and not ...b7-b5 that Black had in mind! His intentions are clear. Black challenges the centre with his d5-pawn and White's options here are similar to those in the French Defence.

Generally now strong White players won't want to trade their e4-pawn for Black's c6-pawn (unless they intend to enter the Panov-Botvinnik Attack – see the next section), but will instead support the e4-pawn with their knight. However, there are two other alternatives here:

a) 3 f3, the aptly named Fantasy Variation is playable, although the problem of the h4-e1 diagonal must be addressed after 3...dxe4 4 fxe5 e5!

b) 3 e5 (yes, the Advance Variation) has its pros and cons. Compared to the French Defence, Black loses a tempo when employing the inevitable ...c6-c5 hit on White's centre, because after all he has moved this c-pawn once already. However, he can use the fact that he has not yet played ...e7-e6 to his advantage by developing his queen's bishop first. Indeed 3...Bf5 is the main continuation here.

3 Nc3

3 Nd2 is also played, with the most likely outcome being a transposition after 3...dxe4.

3...dxe4 4 Nxe4

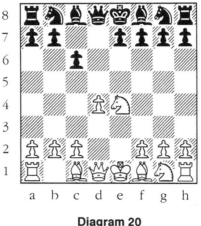

Diagram 20
How can Black develop?

Exercise 13: This is starting position for the main body of Caro-Kann theory. What do you suppose are Black's main options here?

TIP: If you have a space advantage then it is better to avoid exchanges. Looking at it from your opponent's viewpoint; if he is cramped, he would rather exchange off a piece or two in order to leave himself with more room in which to operate.

Centre Counter Defence

1 e4 d5 (Diagram 21)

I must confess that I have trouble understanding the popularity of this opening, which is also known as the Scandinavian Defence. However, it has been employed at the very highest level and so must be taken seriously.

2 exd5

There is no mileage in 2 e5 this time as Black will be able to arrange a good French Defence position by getting in ...Bf5 before ...e7-e6 and ...c7-c5.

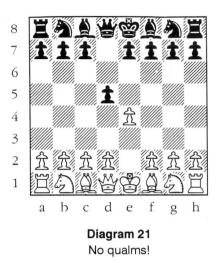

Diagram 21
No qualms!

2...Qxd5

Here Black voluntarily brings his queen into the game. Since this contravenes one of the most basic opening principles, I should here mention that 2...Nf6 probably deserves equal billing. Then after 3 Nc3 Nxd5 4 Nxd5 Qxd5 White lacks a knight with which to attack the centralised queen, so he is better off developing sensibly with moves like Nf3 and d2-d4. The black knight would be well placed on d5, but he will always have to be wary of it being nudged away by c2-c4. With his pawn in the centre, White would have a space advantage but, particularly if he is premature with his c2-c4 advance, there could always be an eventual backlash against the d4-pawn which may become difficult to protect.

 TIP: Often the threat is more dangerous than the execution. With regards the above, the worry for Black of his opponent having the option of c2-c4 is probably greater than if White were to actually implement it.

3 Nc3 Qa5 (Diagram 22)

By sliding the queen over to a5, Black can at least claim to have achieved something. For now the queen is safe, but it must always be on its toes.

4 d4 Nf6 5 Nf3 c6

A flexible continuation, providing an option of blockading the d5-square later and a retreat for the black queen if required.

Remember, the d4-pawn is on a half-open file and is thus a likely future target for the black rooks.

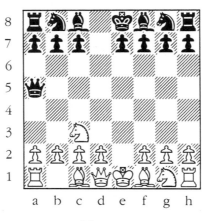

Diagram 22
The black queen – useful, a liability or both!?

6 Bc4 Bf5

Probably even last move you were wondering why Black didn't take the opportunity to pin a knight with ...Bg4. The problem is that 6...Bg4 can be met by 7 h3 Bh5 8 g4 Bg6 9 Ne5. Although White weakens his own kingside, he has a space advantage and a strong knight on e5.

Now I hope you will forgive me from breaking the normal format of this book. I wanted to concentrate specifically on the opening stages of a game, but here I'd like to provide the reader with one of my own encounters. Yes, the whole game. Sorry, but I couldn't resist the temptation!

7 Bd2

Sure, castling kingside with 7 0-0 looks obvious, but the text keeps a discovered attack up White's sleeve and doesn't yet commit the king.

7...e6 8 Qe2

Since this game took place in a simultaneous exhibition, I wanted to be more entertainingly aggressive than usual, and in fact this pawn sacrifice is generally recommended for White in this opening. Black has a very solid position and it takes something a bit special to try and break it down.

Diagram 23
The c2-pawn is poisoned

Delving into specifics, it should be noted here that 8...Bxc2 is extremely risky because of 9 d5! cxd5 10 Nxd5 Qd8 11 Bb5+ Nc6 12 Nxf6+ gxf6 13 Bxc6+ bxc6 14 Qc4 when there is a devastating joint attack on both c6 and c2.

8...Bb4 9 0-0-0 Bxc3?

This was premature, as Black should at least wait until this bishop is attacked. He would be better off continuing his development with 9...Nbd7.

10 Bxc3 Qc7 11 Ne5

Improving the position of the knight to a good central square.

11...0-0

NOTE: 'Pawn storms' are common in situations of opposite-side castling. It is not that the pawns will deliver checkmate themselves, but rather that the firepower of the rooks behind them can be unleashed.

12 g4

White has completed his development and now his attack begins.

12...Be4 13 g5!? (Diagram 24)

Obviously 13 Rhg1 and 13 f3 were alternative candidates, but the text is more adventurous and extremely dangerous. The sacrifice cannot be declined since if the f6-knight were to move, this would let the bishop go for nothing.

13...Bxh1 14 gxf6 Bd5 15 Rg1 (Diagram 25)

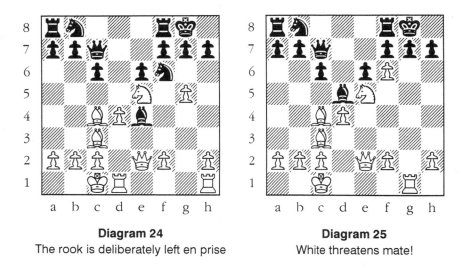

Diagram 24
The rook is deliberately left en prise

Diagram 25
White threatens mate!

Rather than sealing things off with 15 fxg7, White wants to allow his pieces access to the enemy king.

Exercise 14 It is Black's turn, but if were White's, can you spot how he can deliver mate through checks alone?

15...g6

Preventing an invasion of the white rook, but nevertheless giving White an obvious hole on h6 where he can try and invade.

16 Qh5

The queen cannot legally be taken and it is heading for g7 via h6.

16...Nd7

Black must try to remove the f6-pawn as 16...Kh8 17 Qh6 Rg8 18 Rg3 introduces the overwhelming threats of both 19 Rh3 and the more visual 19 Qxh7+ Kxh7 20 Rh3 mate!

17 Ng4

Needless to say my opponent got quite excited here. I could hear murmurings with the insinuations that with the rook pin no longer in force, I had blundered away my queen.

17...gxh5 (Diagram 26)

In fact the last laugh was with me as now there is a delightful combination. Clearly Black shouldn't take the queen, but he did, and now suffers the consequences.

18 Nh6+ Kh8 19 Rg8+! Rxg8 20 Nxf7 mate (Diagram 27)

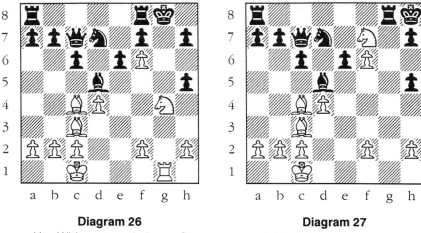

Diagram 26	**Diagram 27**
Has White got carried away?	A knight in shining armour!

Panov-Botvinnik Attack

The Panov-Botvinnik Attack can be reached via transposition from a number of different opening variations, but it is most likely to occur from either the Caro-Kann Defence or the Centre-Counter Defence.

The Caro-Kann move order is

1 e4 c6 2 d4 d5 3 exd5 cxd5 4 c4 Nf6 5 Nc3

and the Centre-Counter move order is

1 e4 d5 2 exd5 Nf6 3 c4 c6

A very sound gambit. If now 4 dxc6 then after 4...Nxc6, Black may be a pawn down, but he has excellent compensation. There is a firm grip over the d4-square with ...e7-e5 and ...Bc5 likely to follow soon. White will have to settle for d2-d3 and a life of misery!

4 d4 cxd5 5 Nc3

Diagram 28
The battle is on for the d5-square

White has a half-open e-file, and he has effectively made another pawn break with c2-c4. The upshot of this is that a trade of Black's d-pawn for this c-pawn will almost certainly result in White being left with an isolated d-pawn.

The immediate 5...dxc4 is inadvisable, as Black will have to withstand some awkward pressure on his f7-sqaure. Black might not wish to lock in his light-squared bishop but in fact that is invariably what he must do in order to maintain a blockade on d5. On 5...g6 for example (hoping to get developed and castled without playing ...e7-e6), 6 Qb3 keeps up the pressure on the black centre. In fact Black is now advised to give White an extra doubled d-pawn (at least for the time being) with 6...Bg7 7 cxd5 0-0 as 6...dxc4 7 Bxc4 forces the ugly 7...e6.

TIP: It is rare that ...g7-g6 and ...e7-e6 are a good combination. More often than not the dark-squared holes created on d6 and f6 make this a poor partnership.

5...e6 6 Nf3 Be7

Preparing to get castled quickly, a feat which can also be achieved by the more adventurous 6...Bb4. There is no justification for placing the bishop on d6, as this would obstruct Black's control of the important d5-square and may also enable White to play c4-c5 with gain of tempo.

7 Bd3

It is always an option for White to play 7 c5. However, although there is no doubt that a queenside majority is desirable in principle, the tension on the centre would then be relieved.

7...dxc4

It makes sense for Black to exchange on c4 once the white bishop has moved.

8 Bxc4 0-0 9 0-0 Nc6

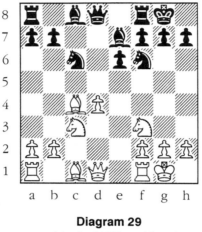

Diagram 29
A typical IQP position

Here we have reached one of the hottest topics of debate in modern chess, the 'Isolated Queen's Pawn' or 'IQP'. If the minor pieces are traded off then the isolated pawn can easily be very weak. However, as it stands the d4-pawn can provide a useful springboard for an attack by the white pieces. Specifically it controls the e5-square, thus keeping Black in his shell. White can hope to used his space advantage to mount an assault against the black king.

Alekhine Defence

1 e4 Nf6

One could hardly call the Alekhine Defence aggressive, and yet immediately Black develops a piece and puts White's centre under attack. An interesting point that I have noticed in junior chess in particular, is that when 1 e4 is at some stage met by ...d7-d5, most player instinctively respond with e4-e5. However, when they are faced with the Alekhine Defence, it is al-

most as though the concept of advancing this pawn is temporarily forgotten and they prefer to defend the pawn passively.
Of course 2 Nc3 is playable, but in order to continue in this
manner, White would have to be prepared to play the Vienna
Game, which would arise by transposition after 2...e5.

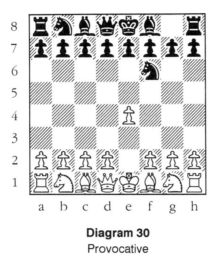

Diagram 30
Provocative

2 e5 Nd5

The only good square for the knight. Whilst 2...Ng8 is safe, it's
an obvious admission that Black has made a mistake. He must
of course tread very carefully here. We have already seen how
knights can end up in hot water in open spaces and after say
2...Ne4 3 d3 Nc5 4 d4 Ne4 5 f3 it would already be the end of
the line for this stray steed.

3 d4

As usual there is plenty of choice here, but you can never go far
wrong putting a pawn in the centre.

3...d6

Now Black strikes back at the white centre. White can go for
broke on the space front with 4 c4 Nb6 5 f4 (the Four Pawns
Variation), but there are naturally risks involved.

**WARNING: Whilst Black has to be careful not to get his knight
trapped, White must avoid over-extending himself to the point
where his pawns drop off.**

4 Nf3

A conservative approach. Now Black will try to chisel away at the white centre, but as long as White keeps it intact he will retain an initiative.

4...Bg4 5 Be2 e6 6 0-0

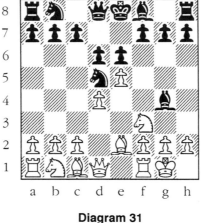

Diagram 31
A pleasant space advantage.

White can play c2-c4 when he feels the time is right.

Pirc Defence

1 e4 d6

At first glance this is as unimpressive as 1...e6, but the pawn on d6 fulfils a critical role.

2 d4 Nf6 3 Nc3

Note that 3 e5 is unrealistically ambitious now due to 3...dxe5 4 dxe5 Qxd1+ 5 Kxd1 Ng4 with a pawn-winning fork.

3...g6 (Diagram 32)

And here we have the Pirc Defence, which is distinguishable from the closely related Modern Defence only in that Black has placed a priority on developing his king's knight. A typical sequence for the Modern Defence is 1 e4 g6 2 d4 Bg7 3 Nc3 c6 4 f4 b5 5 Nf3 (see Diagram 33), when Black is delaying his development until the last possible moment. This creates extra options for Black but he must be careful not to neglect the development of his kingside pieces completely!

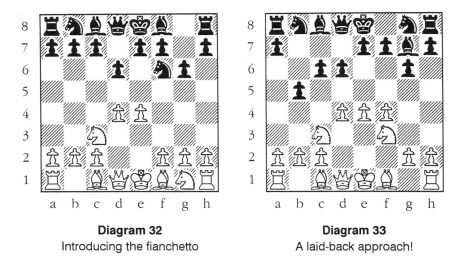

Diagram 32
Introducing the fianchetto

Diagram 33
A laid-back approach!

In more recent times a weird idea in the form of 1 e4 d6 2 d4 Nf6 3 Nc3 c6 (the Pribyl System) has become quite popular. Remarkably, even strong players have been known to dabble with the black pieces after 4 f4 (hardly forced, but why shouldn't White take time out to expand?) 4...Qa5 5 Bd3 e5. Frankly though, this looks very suspect to me.

After the standard 3...g6 Black uses his bishop to provide some latent pressure against the white centre. Black is prepared to give up the centre for the moment, preferring to wait until he feels the time is right to attack it (often with ...e7-e5 or ...c7-c5).

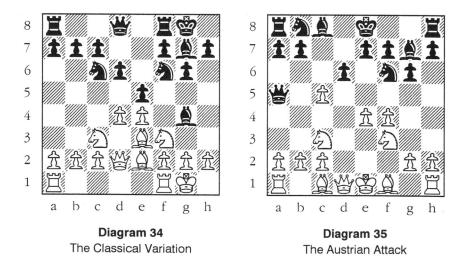

Diagram 34
The Classical Variation

Diagram 35
The Austrian Attack

White himself has a variety of different ways to tackle this opening and here we see a number of common positions that can arise.

If White opts to develop quietly with 4 Nf3 Bg7 5 Be2 0-0 6 0-0, then we reach what is known as the Classical Variation. Play may continue 6...Bg4 7 Be3 Nc6 8 Qd2 e5 reaching the position in Diagram 34.

A sharper idea for White is the Austrian Attack 4 f4 Bg7 5 Nf3, when Black often chooses to counter with 5...c5 6 dxc5 Qa5 with a dual threat of ...Nxe4 and ...Qxc5, as in Diagram 35.

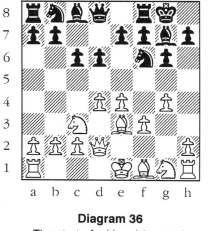

Diagram 36
The start of a kingside attack

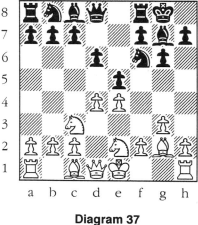

Diagram 37
Anything you can do ...

Alternatively, White can try to build up an attack with 4 Be3 Bg7 5 f3 0-0 6 Qd2 c6 7 g4 with h2-h4 in mind (Diagram 36).

Finally, White can undertake his own fianchetto with 4 g3 Bg7 5 Bg2 0-0 6 Nge2 (Diagram 37).

 NOTE: Remember that there are often different set-ups available in a given opening. It's certainly not always clear that one is better than another, and more often than not it simply boils down to a matter of taste.

Nimzowitsch Defence

1 e4 Nc6

There is no doubt that the Nimzowitsch Defence is comparatively offbeat, and in fact it is rarely employed outside of club level chess. It's not as though the move 1...Nc6 prevents a second pawn from making it into the centre

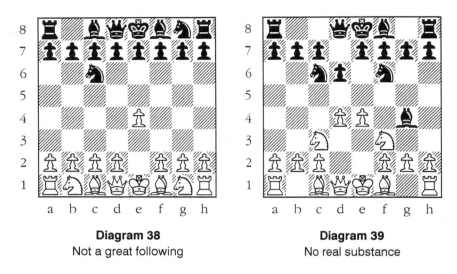

Diagram 38
Not a great following

Diagram 39
No real substance

2 d4 d6

Black can also play 2...e5 here, but the main alternative is 2....d5, which bares a vague resemblance to the Centre-Counter if White co-operates with 3 exd5 Qxd5. However, Black has hindered himself from playing the ...c7-c5 pawn break, so 3 e5 is quite playable, whilst the sharp 3 Nc3 dxe4 4 d5 is quite interesting.

3 Nf3 Nf6 4 Nc3 Bg4

It's clear what Black is up to: putting pressurise on the white d4-pawn. However, whilst it's commendable to develop the pieces so quickly, the reality is that this is rarely successful unless the pawns are involved too. White can avoid ...Bxf3 (when he'd have to recapture with the g-pawn) more than satisfactorily with 5 Be2, 5 Be3 or 5 Bb5.

Summary

When deciding on whether to trade pawns, remember that effectively you will be swapping your pawn doing the initial taking with the enemy one doing the *replacing*.

When the centre is blocked, there isn't quite the same urgency to castle.

If you have a space advantage then it is better to avoid fair swaps. Looking at it from your opponent's viewpoint; if he is cramped, he would rather exchange off a piece or two in order to leave himself with more room in which to operate.

Often the threat is more dangerous than the execution. It is rare that ...g7-g6 and ...e7-e6 are a good combination. More often than not the dark-squared holes created on d6 and f6 make a poor partnership.

Chapter Four

Symmetrical d-pawn Openings

- Veresov System ■ London System
- Queen's Gambit Declined
- Queen's Gambit Accepted ■ Slav Defence
- Semi-Slav Defence
- Catalan System ■ Chigorin
- Albin Counter-Gambit

Essentially when one thinks of 1 d4 d5, there is only one challenging variation that springs to mind, the Queen's Gambit, 2 c4.

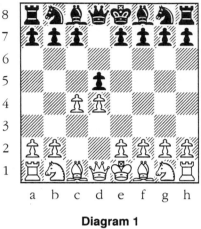

Diagram 1
The Queen's Gambit

Sticking rigidly to opening principles, White should theoretically be planning a way to achieve central domination. Realistically though there is no practical way that White will be able to get in e2-e4 whilst there is a black pawn on d5. Note that unlike 1 e4 e5 systems, the queen does not help out in that department and there is a black knight and light-squared bishop ready to come to squares that will keep the e4-square firmly in Black's grip.

Hence, the Queen's Gambit is the Grandmaster's choice. It makes a thematic pawn break and attempts to lure Black's d5-pawn away. Before I tackle this giant of an opening in earnest though, let me skip through a few of the less testing alternatives.

Veresov System

1 d4 d5 2 Nc3

White gets straight to the point and hopes to play 3 e4. Of course Black could aim for a transposition into the French Defence or the Caro-Kann with 2...e6 or 2...c6 respectively, but there is no reason for him not to be stubborn.

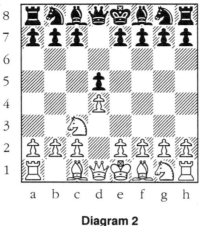

Diagram 2
Lacking in subtlety

2...Nf6

Preventing White's aforementioned plan. The same position could easily be reached via 1 d4 Nf6 2 Nc3 d5.

3 Bg5 Nbd7

The logical decision. Black prevents the doubling of his pawns without playing 3...e6. In itself that wouldn't be the end of the world, but since the knight is pinned, White could then play 4 e4, transposing to the French Defence.

4 f3

Diagram 3
Eager for that big pawn centre

White plays relentlessly in the pursuit of e2-e4, but nonetheless this move deprives the king's knight of its natural square and creates the odd hole (i.e. e3 and f2).

4...c5!

Black wants to avoid allowing his opponent to consolidate a big centre and so acts quickly with his own pawn break. Now White has something else to think about and if he captures on c5 he will be exposed along the b6-g1 diagonal.

5 e4 cxd4 6 Qxd4 e5 7 Qa4 d4

Diagram 4
White lacks co-ordination

White's direct, but irregular opening play has backfired a little – it is Black who holds the aces in the middle of the board!

 TIP: In queen's pawn openings it is generally advisable not to obstruct one's c-pawn, which can be used either to attack the opponent's centre or to defend one's own.

London System

1 d4 d5 2 Nf3

It is certainly difficult to fault this move, especially as it doesn't preclude c2-c4 as a future possibility.

2...Nf6 3 Bf4

This is the characteristic move of the London System. White's intended piece set-up is shown in Diagram 5.

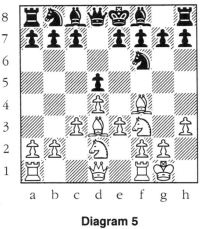

Diagram 5
Not so ambitious

Sure, Black will have a few moves as well, but White usually seems to play these moves regardless. His pieces seem to fit in nicely and if there is a drawback it's that potential rook action isn't exactly at a premium. In fact generally it is Black that makes the pawn break with ...c7-c5, thus leaving him holding the cards as to which open/half-open files should be created.

A similar idea can be adopted with the bishop on g5. That is known as the Torre Attack and is covered in the next chapter.

Queen's Gambit Accepted

1 d4 d5 2 c4 dxc4

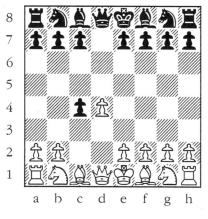

Diagram 6
I'll have that, thanks!

NOTE: The Queen's Gambit isn't strictly speaking really a gambit at all, as Black is unable to keep his extra pawn.

With regards the above note, let's take a look at what might happen if Black stubbornly refuses to give back the pawn, starting with one of White's main options here; 3 e3. Well, Black can cement the pawn with 3...b5 and then rather than just developing, White should act quickly to undermine this protection with 4 a4.

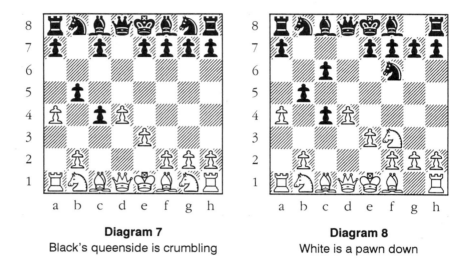

Diagram 7
Black's queenside is crumbling

Diagram 8
White is a pawn down

It soon becomes apparent that although Black needs to maintain a pawn on b5 in order to cling on to his c4-pawn, in fact that just isn't possible. The a-pawn would be pinned, so 4...a6 doesn't help, while 4...c6 5 axb5 cxb5 6 Qf3 is rather embarrassing. This last trick may seem 'lucky', but in fact if the two king's knights were already developed, say after 3 Nf3 Nf6 4 e3 b5 5 a4, there would still be another way to place Black under pressure.

Exercise 15 Can you spot what White should play in Diagram 8?

I have seen many a junior chuckle when seeing his opponent accept the Queen's Gambit, suggesting that it is simply a mistake. It's true that it does appear to give White a free run in the centre, but that is hardly the end of the story. Take the most obvious continuation:

3 e4

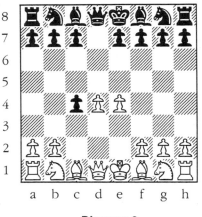

Diagram 9
An attractive pawn centre

Ultimately this is what White is angling for in the Queen's Gambit Accepted, a double pawn centre. However, although White has achieved a delightful centre, the fact that he has not yet regained the c-pawn offers Black the opportunity to launch a counter offensive.

3...e5

This and 3...c5 both give White something to think about. The point is that 4 dxe5 Qxd1+ 5 Kxd1 is certainly not favourable for White. It's not clear that either side will lose their 'extra' doubled pawn and it is the white monarch that is the most inconvenienced. However, 4 d5 is little better as after 4...Nf6 5 Nc3, 5...b5 is possible because White has his e4-pawn to think about.

White should play 4 Nf3 when there are all sorts of things going on in the centre.

The above sharp variation is why many players prefer to side-step the possibility of ...e7-e5 with:

3 Nf3 Nf6 4 e3

As we have seen, 4...b5 isn't wise and so this is a safe approach for White to adopt. White will develop his pieces with the idea of playing e3-e4 later on. Here Black can excavate his bishop (before playing ...e7-e6), but must be careful after 4...Bg4 5 Bxc4.

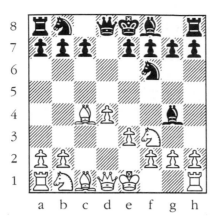

Diagram 10
Can you spot White's threat?

Exercise 16 What is White threatening here?

 WARNING: Never lose your sense of danger. Remain optimistic, but remember your opponent can have threats!

Instead of 4...Bg4, it is safer to play

4...e6

Black has alternative plans for his c8-bishop.

5 Bxc4 c5

Black is prepared to fight for a fair share of the central action.

6 0-0 a6

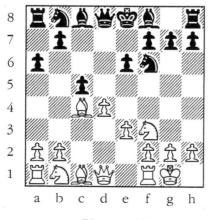

Diagram 11
The move ...b7-b5 is on the cards

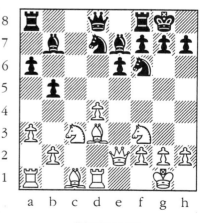

Diagram 12
A typical IQP position

Black intends an expansion on the queenside where he will fianchetto his light-squared bishop. A typical position that could arise is depicted in Diagram 12 where we see another IQP situation in action.

Queen's Gambit Declined

1 d4 d5 2 c4 e6 3 Nc3

White pressurises the d5-pawn. Here Black can immediately strike out at White's centre with 3...c5, which is known as the Tarrasch Variation. The drawback of this line is that Black often ends up with an isolated queen's pawn with White's dark-squared bishop not locked in, so most Grandmasters prefer the more restrained

3...Nf6

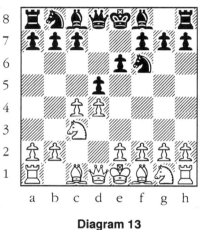

Diagram 13
Black bolsters the centre

I suppose logically anything that is not accepting the gambit, must really be declining it! However, when we refer to the Queen's Gambit Declined, images similar to the above are conjured up. Black has supported his d5-pawn with another pawn, so that c4xd5 can always be met by e6xd5. However, this leads to an imbalance in which White will have a half-open c-file with Black the corresponding e-file. Although it is usually at White's discretion when this trade is made, it should be noted that Black has not ruled out ...d5xc4 entirely and could easily employ it later.

4 Bg5 Be7

Unpinning the knight and thus relieving some of the pressure on d5. Clearly 4...dxc4 5 e4 is not what Black is after, but what about 4...Nbd7 instead?

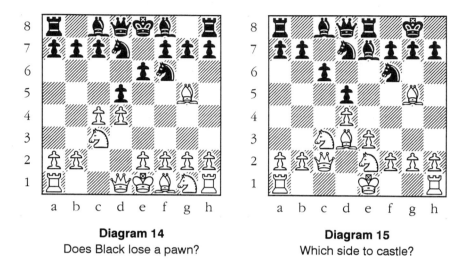

Diagram 14
Does Black lose a pawn?

Diagram 15
Which side to castle?

Exercise 17: The d7-square looks like a sensible place for the knight (remember that rule about not obstructing the c-pawn in queen's pawn openings), but in the above position does Black lose a pawn?

5 e3 0-0 6 Nf3

As always there are several variations within an opening. If White chooses to enter the Exchange Variation with 6 exd5 cxd5 7 Bd3 c6 8 Qc2 Nbd7 9 Nge2 Re8, then the position in Diagram 15 would have been reached:

The white knight is on e2 rather than f3, but as with many things in chess, this placement is a matter of taste. White has several very reasonable plans. He can castle kingside and launch a 'minority attack' (utilising his b-pawn with b2-b4-b5 to try and weaken Black's queenside pawn structure) or he can aim to get a big centre with f2-f3 and e3-e4. Alternatively White could castle queenside and attempt a kingside attack. With the black knight slotting nicely into f8 whatever, at least Black has no problems with his often troublesome light-squared bishop.

6...b6

Here Black takes matters into his own hands and searches out a new diagonal for his bishop.

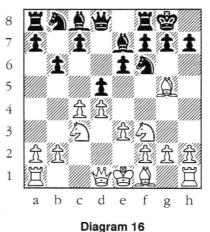

Diagram 16
A ...c7-c5 break is also supported

With his bishop headed for b7, Black now the option of meeting c4xd5 with ...Nxd5.

Slav Defence

1 d4 d5 2 d4 c6

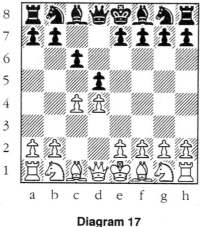

Diagram 17
The c8-bishop is not obstructed

This time Black supports his d-pawn with the c-pawn. White can now behave in a dull manner by trading pawns, thus obtaining a symmetrical position but with him to move. However, this rather unambitious Exchange Variation is not generally popular, as most White players prefer to keep the tension for a while longer.

 WARNING: White must be careful now as he has to be sure that he is prepared for Black taking on c4 and then trying to protect it with ...b7-b5. Compared to the QGA, Black has now already played ...c7-c6.

3 Nf3

3 Nc3 is also playable, but this has gone out of fashion because this knight can get in the way after 3...dxc4 4 e4 b5 5 a4 b4.

3...Nf6 4 Nc3

Now or on the last turn White could also opt to play the more cautious 4 e3. Then he never has to fear ...d5xc4 and he remains in control of the tension situation on c4 and d5. However, the obvious drawback is that it locks in his dark-squared bishop.

4...dxc4 (Diagram 18)

The main advantage of the Slav over the Queen's Gambit Declined is that the c8-bishop is not hindered by a pawn on e6. However, he can't bring it out just like that. The problem is 4...Bf5 5 cxd5 cxd5 6 Qb3! when there is no satisfactory way of defending the b7-pawn given that Black has to guard d5 as well.

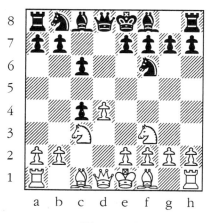

Diagram 18
The Main Line Slav

One comparatively new approach for Black is 4...a6. At first it seems hard to believe that a pawn move such as this should be acceptable so early in the game. However, the simple idea is that Black wants to solve the problem of his b-pawn and simultaneously hurry White's decision-making along with ...b7-b5. Only then he will be able to develop his bishop safely.

5 a4

An important concept. Rather than waiting for ...b7-b5 and then beginning the hard work of undermining this pawn, White nips the whole idea in the bud straight away.

5...Bf5

Meanwhile Black gets his bishop out and prevents 6 e4.

6 e3

The difference in playing this move now is that there is no longer a black pawn on d5 and so White can hope to force e3-e4 later. A more direct approach is 6 Ne5, with the aggressive f2-f3 and e2-e4 in mind.

6...e6 7 Bxc4 Bb4

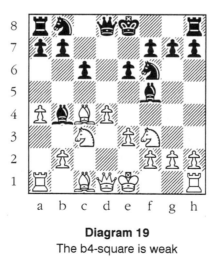

Diagram 19
The b4-square is weak

The theoretical position above invokes much discussion. With his good control of d5 and comfortably developed pieces, Black is very solid. However, although Black has rather annoyingly (from White's point of view) made the b4-square a home for his bishop, White can always argue that the potential of his extra centre pawn gives him the upper hand. Indeed should he ever be able to arrange e3-e4 and e4-e5, then it would be difficult to argue with him.

Semi-Slav Defence

1 d4 d5 2 c4 e6

This and Black's next move are interchangeable, although this move order has the advantage of avoiding the possibility of the notoriously boring Exchange Variation of the Slav.

3 Nc3 c6

On the face of it this looks rock solid, but is Black possibly overdoing it on the supporting of the d5-pawn? Well, appearances can be deceptive. Take a look at some positions that are indigenous to this fascinating defence:

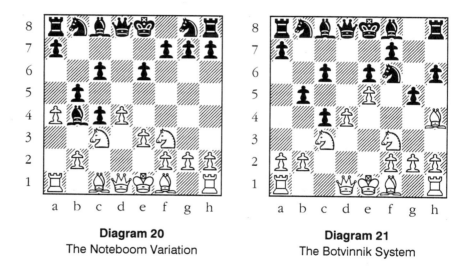

Diagram 20
The Noteboom Variation

Diagram 21
The Botvinnik System

The sharp gambit variation seen in Diagram 20 arises after 4 Nf3 dxc4 5 e3 b5 6 a4 Bb4. Black is clinging to his extra pawn, indirectly using the pin on the knight. White will have to utilise the undermining b2-b3 somehow and the continuation 7 Bd2 Bb7 8 axb5 Bxc3 9 Bxc3 cxb5 10 b3 a5 11 bxc4 b4 is incredibly double-edged. White has the extra centre pawns and the bishop pair, but Black's a- and b-pawns provide him with a headache.

In Diagram 21 we see another gambit variation, known as the

Botvinnik System, which arises after 4 Nf3 Nf6 5 Bg5 dxc4 6 e4 b5 7 e5 h6 8 Bh4 g5. Black has secured a scary queenside pawn mass, but there is also much action on the kingside and 9 Nxg5 hxg5 10 Bxg5 Nbd7 11 exf6 leads to a crazy position which has been the subject of numerous Grandmaster games.

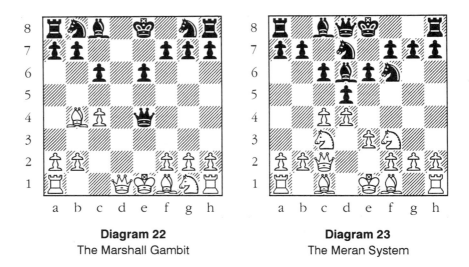

Diagram 22
The Marshall Gambit

Diagram 23
The Meran System

After 4 e4 dxe4 5 Nxe4 Qxd4 6 Bb4 Qxe4+ (Diagram 22) White sacrifices at least one pawn, but the absence of a key black bishop means that White gets plenty of compensation on the dark squares.

After 4 Nf3 Nf6 5 e3 Nbd7 6 Qc2 Bd6 (Diagram 23) we have a bit of peace and quiet! White may later seek to free his dark-squared bishop through e3-e4, with Black considering a timely ...e6-e5 or ...c6-c5 (with or without ...dxc4).

WARNING: At first the Semi-Slav may look innocuous, but be warned, there is a sting in the tail!

Catalan System

1 d4 d5 2 c4 e6 3 Nf3 Nf6 4 g3

Strictly speaking, this is a kind of Queen's Gambit Declined, although the difference here is that White decides that he wants a change of diagonal for his king's bishop. It seems odd to seek a fianchetto when the bishop is the obvious candidate for protecting/recapturing on c4, but it transpires that there are other volunteers for that job.

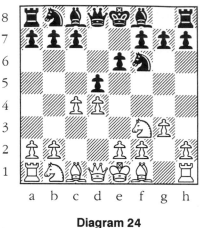

Diagram 24
Still not a gambit

4...Be7 5 Bg2

The bishop can be extremely useful pressurising Black's queenside in this manner.

5...0-0 6 0-0 dxc4

Moves like ...c7-c6 and ...Nbd7 are not on for Black, as he could get lumbered with an exceedingly grim light-squared bishop.

7 Qc2

7 Ne5 is the other often utilised method of regaining the pawn.

7...a6 8 Qxc4 b5

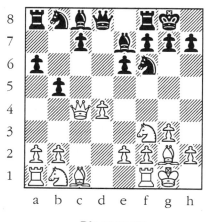

Diagram 25
Black will be able to develop his bishop

The point behind Black's last move. He needs the tempo gained on the white queen in order to contest the a8-h1 diagonal. As well as 9...Bb7, Black will be looking to ultimately get in ...c7-c5 so that this pawn isn't so vulnerable on the half-open c-file.

Chigorin Defence

1 d4 d5 2 c4 Nc6

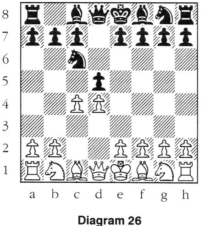

Diagram 26
Who likes defending?

Truthfully I would have to say that I believe the Chigorin Defence to be positionally flawed – it's anti-positional to block the c-pawn with a knight. However, the tactical resources at Black's disposal make it a tough nut to crack.

3 cxd5

Naturally both 3 Nc3 and 3 Nf3 are sensible, but I suppose the acid test is to question Black's reluctance to support his centre.

3...Qxd5 4 e3

TIP: Even if your long-term intention is to play e2-e4, often it is more prudent to settle on a halfway house (e2-e3) and to finish your development before realising your ambition.

4...e5

A simple development of the pieces will be of no use to Black, as he lacks a pawn foothold in the centre. He would no doubt be overrun in the middle and so wisely maintains his pressure on d4.

5 Nc3 Bb4

If the queen moves then White could advance with d4-d5.

6 Bd2 Bxc3 7 bxc3

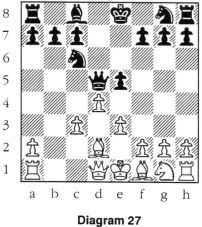

Diagram 27
Black has mixed things up!

White has the latent power of the two bishops and his centre has great potential too.

Albin Counter-Gambit

1 d4 d5 2 c4 e5

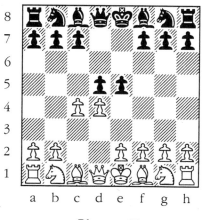

Diagram 28
Can you be serious?

Well, I didn't think that this chapter would be complete without a genuine gambit. Here Black takes the 'place your pawns in the centre' rule very literally by offering his e-pawn as a sacrifice to achieve speedy development.

3 dxe5 d4 4 Nf3

Not falling into the famous trap 4 e3? Bb4+ 5 Bd2 dxe3 6 Bxb4 exf2+ 7 Ke2 fxg1N+!!, when Black nets at least a piece in view of 8 Rxg1 Bg4+.

4...Nc6 5 g3

The simplest way to complete the kingside development, side-stepping all of the complications.

5...Be6 6 Nbd2 Qd7 7 Bg2 0-0-0

Diagram 29
Worth an outing?

If it weren't for the fact that Black is a pawn down, I would have to say that he has a good position. He is nicely centralised and at the same time has reasonable chances for a kingside attack. Mind you, White can launch an offensive against Black's queenside and after all, a pawn is a pawn!

NOTE: You will occasionally hear or read apparently mindless remarks such as 'a pawn is a pawn'. They are purely meant as a reminder that without going over the top – it is generally advisable to be a little materialistic.

Summary

In queen's pawn openings it is generally advisable not to obstruct one's c-pawn, which can be used either to attack the opponent's centre or to defend one's own.

Even if your long-term intention is to play e2-e4, often it is more prudent to settle on a halfway house (e2-e3) and to finish your development before realising your ambition.

Chapter Five

Other Defences to 1 d4

- Trompowsky Attack ■ Torre Attack
- Colle System ■ Nimzo-Indian Defence
- Queen's Indian Defence ■ Dutch Defence
- King's Indian Defence
- Modern Benoni
- Grünfeld Defence
- Old Indian Defence
- Budapest Gambit

For the majority of this chapter I will be concentrating on deviations after the starting moves 1 d4 Nf6.

Diagram 1
Black stops 2 e4

With his first move Black finds an alternative to 1...d5 that fulfils the same function of preventing 2 e4. For those who may wonder why 2 c4 is so popular now, let me remind you that if White attempts to force through e2-e4 with 2 Nc3, then Black can employ 2...d5, transposing to the Veresov System, which we have already covered. White soon discovers that there are no easy pawn breaks on offer, whilst Black still has ...c7-c5.

The specific purpose of 2 c4 then (other than to gain space) is to dissuade a future ...d7-d5 or at least make it so that this wouldn't halt White's e2-e4 ambitions.

Before we get involved in this interesting debate, let me first just eliminate one or two other club chess favourites.

Trompowsky Attack

1 d4 Nf6 2 Bg5

Although this breaks the rule of 'knights before bishops', White immediately pressurises the developed black knight. The big question is whether or not he is prepared to trade on f6 after, say, 2...d5. That would concede a bishop for knight, but would also double Black's pawns. Whilst it's far from clear that this is good for White, generally most Black players prefer to avoid this breaching of their pawn structure.

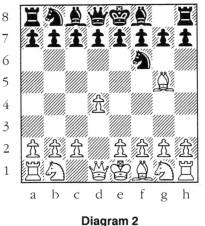

Diagram 2
Bishop before knight!

2...e6

This sets up a self-pin and for that reason the alternative 2...Ne4 is also popular. Whilst it's a second knight move, White is obliged to move his bishop again, either to f4 or h4. Then Black can choose between the solid 3...d5 or the sharper 3...c5.

3 e4 h6 4 Bxf6

The pin would be no longer in effect after 4 Bh4 g5, and thus the e4-pawn would be up for grabs.

4...Qxf6 5 Nf3 d6 6 Nc3

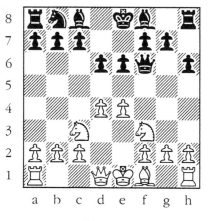

Diagram 3
Cramped but with the bishop pair

TIP: Generally knights prefer blocked positions, with bishops relishing the open board.

Although this tip implies that a future ...e6-e5, d4-d5 wouldn't favour Black as he is the one with the two bishops, note that White's remaining bishop would be a bad one.

TIP: When you only have one bishop, try to advance your pawns onto the opposite-coloured squares from your remaining bishop. That way they work in tandem, rather than duplicating coverage of the same squares.

It follows that you should to try to lure enemy pawns to the same colour as an opponent's remaining bishop. This explains why aiming for ...e6-e5 is more logical here than aiming for ...d6-d5.

Torre Attack

1 d4 Nf6 2 Nf3 e6 3 Bg5

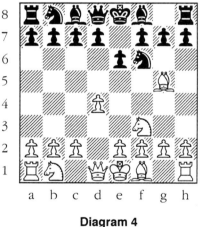

Diagram 4
Popular with club players

At first sight the Torre Attack is very similar to the Trompowsky in that White might be seeking to play a quick e2-e4. option. In practical play though it is a system very much in the mould of the London System. White has a specific piece configuration in mind and is rarely swayed from it.

4...c5

Giving White something to think about. It's worth noting that after the illogical 5 dxc5? Bxc5, Black would threaten 6...Bxf2+ 7 Kxf2 Ne4+. The quieter 4...h6 5 Bxf6 (5 Bh4 is also possible) 5...Qxf6 6 e4 would transpose to the Trompowsky.

5 e3

It's no great surprise that White is inclined to maintain his centre; 5 c3 is also very sensible.

5...cxd4 6 exd4 b6

The fianchetto of Black's queen's bishop is a common occurrence in lines where he plays ...e7-e6, as after all the bishop does not have a great future on the c8-h3 diagonal.

7 Bd3 Bb7 8 0-0 Be7 9 Nbd2 0-0

Both sides develop in a simple and solid fashion.

10 c3 d6

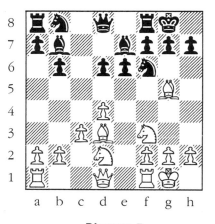

Diagram 5
The pawn on d6 prevents Ne5

Although it could be argued that c2-c3 (as opposed to c2-c4) isn't very ambitious, White can try to attack Black's queenside structure with his a-pawn. Although White also has some chances for a kingside attack, Black is very solid and the pawn on d6 frustrates White's ambitions of utilising the e5-square.

A similar set-up can be used against a black kingside fianchetto.

1 d4 Nf6 2 Nf3 g6 3 Bg5 Bg7 4 e3 0-0 5 Nbd2 d6 6 c3

Here White seems intent on blunting the enemy bishop:

Diagram 6
Black should aim for ...e7-e5 or ...c7-c5

Colle System

1 d4 Nf6 2 e3

This is another favourite in weekend congress-style chess, but certainly at this juncture it looks a little daft! White gives up on e2-e4 for a while and shuts in his own bishop on c1, though again there is a particular set-up that White has in mind.

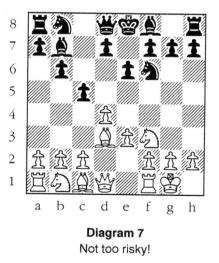

Diagram 7
Not too risky!

The solid way for White to play is 2...e6 3 Nf3 c5 4 Bd3 Bb7 5 0-0, as in Diagram 7. Here White could be ultra-solid with 6 c3, but frankly that looks like overkill. More likely he should go for c2-c4, which can be prepared by 6 b3 with Bb2 and Nbd2 to follow.

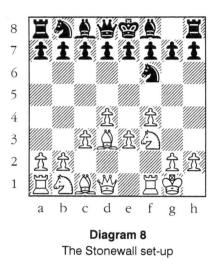

Diagram 8
The Stonewall set-up

Here we see a set-up that is often used by Black in the Dutch Defence (covered in a later section). Sure, I've not exactly been generous in giving Black moves, but that's because there are quite a few different ways for him to react. Should he just settle for playing the likes of ...e7-e6 and ...d7-d5, then White often invokes caveman simplicity, plonking his knight on e5 and then swinging the rook up (to f3) and along (to h3) with (assuming Black has castled kingside) a remarkably dangerous kingside attack.

TIP: Against Stonewall type set-ups (where the opponent has played f2-f4 or ...f7-f5) it is generally suggested that fianchettoing the king's bishop is a good idea. This helps to prevent the f-pawn from advancing further and means that any bishop pointing towards h7 (or h2) is 'biting on granite' (i.e. a g6- or g3-pawn).

Nimzo-Indian Defence

1 d4 Nf6 2 c4 e6 3 Nc3 Bb4

The highly regarded Nimzo-Indian Defence halts White's plans for progress in the centre without having to transpose to playing ....d7-d5, as in the Queen's Gambit Declined. The early battle in this opening is all about the e4-square and invariably the game becomes imbalanced when Black is forced to give up his bishop for the c3-knight. If this involves White getting doubled c-pawns then some fascinating positions emerge in which White has the advantage of the two bishops, but at the cost of a damaged pawn structure.

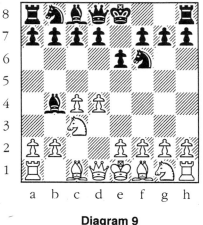

Diagram 9
The pin helps prevent 4 e4

White has numerous options here, but take a look at some interesting theoretical positions:

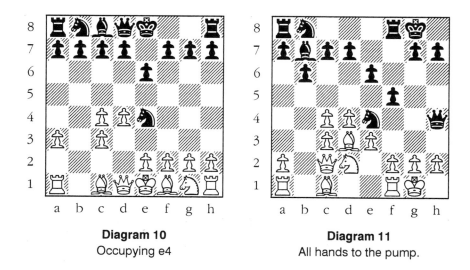

Diagram 10
Occupying e4

Diagram 11
All hands to the pump.

Diagram 10 could arise if White were to challenge the bishop immediately with 4 a3 Bxc3 5 bxc3, and Black went for the ambitious 5...Ne4. The knight can't capture on c3 because it would have no escape route after Qc2. However, it's not easy for White to budge this annoying knight as 6 f3 runs into 6...Qh4+ 7 g3 Nxg3.

In Diagram 11 we see a position that can arise after the moves 4 e3 b6 5 Bd3 Bb7 6 Nf3 Ne4 7 Qc2 f5 8 0-0 Bxc3 9 bxc3 0-0 10 Nd2 Qh4. Again the black knight sits nicely in the middle. White tries to eject it, but his opponent uses all available resource to keep it there.

Exercise 18 Were White to try 11 g3 in the above position, how should Black react?

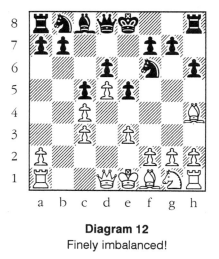

Diagram 12
Finely imbalanced!

After the moves 4 Bg5 h6 5 Bh4 c5 7 d5 Bxc3+ 8 bxc3 d6 9 e3 e5 we see a typical blocked position in which the battle will revolve around whether White can utilise his two bishops against the two knights. The black knights would prefer it if the position were to remain closed, and the doubled c-pawns are potential targets. However, the f6-pin can be a tricky one to negotiate, as ...g7-g5 gives White more potential pawn break options on the kingside.

TIP: If the characteristic Nimzo-Indian doubled c-pawns emerge, it often makes sense for Black to target the one on c4 as it can't easily be protected by a rook. It is often worth considering a plan involving getting a bishop to a6 and a knight to a5.

Diagram 13
The pressurising fianchetto

After the moves 4 Nf3 c5 5 g3 cxd4 6 Nxd4 0-0 7 Bd2 d5 8 Qb3 Bxc3+ 9 Qxc3 e5 10 Nb3 d4 White has secured the two bishops and has some pressure on Black's queenside. Nevertheless, Black has comfortable development thanks to his handy centre pawns.

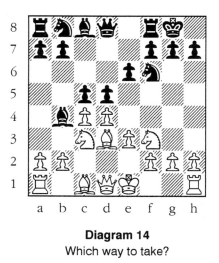

Diagram 14
Which way to take?

Here we see a common position after the sequence 4 e3 0-0 5 Nf3 d5 6 Bd3 c5. The situation in the centre is confusing with plenty of possible pawn trades. In fact a typical IQP (Isolated Queen's Pawn) position often occurs when the white d4-pawn is the last one left standing in the centre!

Diagram 15
The Classical Variation (4 Qc2) involves early queen moves

White has obtained the bishop pair without having to have his pawn structure damaged via the moves 4 Qc2 d5 5 a3 Bxc3+ 6 Qxc3 Ne4 7 Qc2 c5. However, this has taken time and Black can use his lead in development to cause early problems.

Queen's Indian Defence

1 d4 Nf6 2 c4 e6 3 Nf3

3 Nf3, not allowing the Nimzo-Indian, is an easy developing move. However, this is not as forcing as 4 e4 isn't a threat.

3...b6

Diagram 16
Black has the e4-square very much in mind

At this point Black still has options of returning to the Queen's Gambit Declined with 3...d5 or aiming for a Modern Benoni with the attacking 3...c5 (read on!).

Whilst I have to say that the bishop fianchetto is extremely logical, the Bogo-Indian , 3...Bb4+, demonstrates that there is another solution to getting it developed. This could transpose to a Nimzo-Indian after 4 Nc3, but it would be more consistent for White to interpose something (but not the queen!) on d2.

After say 4 Bd2, one possible variation is 4...Qe7 5 g3 0-0 6 Bg2 Bxd2+ 7 Qxd2 d6 8 Nc3 e5, reaching the position in Diagram 17.

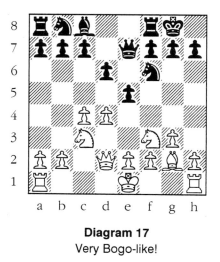

Diagram 17
Very Bogo-like!

Here White retains a slight space advantage, but having traded off his dark-squared bishop, Black very sensibly creates a dark-squared pawn chain. It naturally follows that his bishop is then provided with possibilities along the c8-h3 diagonal.

After the Queen's Indian move, 3...b6, a quiet game often arises after White challenges the long diagonal with his own kingside fianchetto with 4 g3. The main alternative though is 4 a3 which brings to mind that old chestnut.

 WARNING: Beware making unnecessary pawn moves.

The above warning wisely suggests that in the opening it is better to get on with your piece development rather than making pawn moves on the side which achieve comparatively little in the overall scheme of things. It could prove disastrous to get caught in the opening with few members of your army ready to do battle.

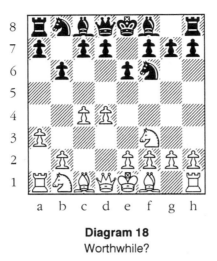

Diagram 18
Worthwhile?

The big question is whether it is worth spending a move on 4 a3 to secure the knight on c3. I guess the answer is that many top players think that it is worth a tempo, clearly valuing the elimination of ...Bb4 quite highly.

TIP: Although ...b7-b6 would imply that ...Bb7 will follow next, in fact often in the Queen's Indian ...Ba6 is a valuable commodity as it is useful for trying to embarrass White's c4-pawn.

An interesting possibility for Black in the Queen's Indian Defence is to meet 4 g3 or 4 a3 with 4...Ba6 rather than the standard 4...Bb7.

Dutch Defence

1 d4 f5

So far in this chapter I have been at pains to emphasise the need for Black to try and fight for control of the e4-square, so it only makes sense that I should use this opportunity to discuss another controversial opening, 1...f5, the Dutch Defence.

No doubt it may cross the reader's mind that the above diagram depicts a Sicilian Defence, but on the opposite side of the board! However, since 1...f5 exposes the king along the h5-e8 diagonal, I would have to say that this is definitely where the resemblance ends.

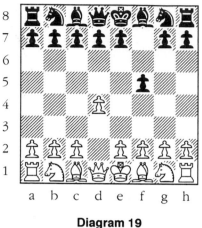

Diagram 19
A bold defence

Recalling the advice that I offered in the section on the Colle and Stonewall sections, 2 g3 now is both sensible and popular, although Black isn't compelled to concede an outpost on e5 by playing ...d7-d5. Indeed the Dutch Leningrad sees 2...Nf6 3 Bg2 g6 3 Nf3 Bg7 4 0-0 0-0 5 c4 d6 6 Nc3, as in Diagram 20.

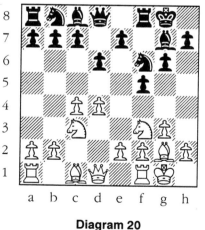

Diagram 20
White adopts a positional approach

Here there is still a tussle going on over the e4-square. White would like to either get in e2-e4 or else d4-d5 and Nd4. The e6-square is a clear weak point and if possible, Black would love to free himself with ...e7-e5.

With such a provocative move as 1...f5 there are bound to be some tactical responses. One of those is 2 e4 (the Staunton Gambit), but let me highlight another common attempt at refutation:

2 Bg5

This move is designed to throw a spanner in the works. White justifies developing a bishop before a knight by preventing the natural 2...Nf6. Well, actually that move is still possible, but after 3 Bxf6 exf6 4 e3, there is little doubt who has the easier game. The f5-pawn is a clear target.

2...g6

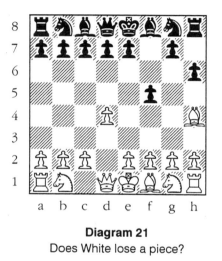

Diagram 21
Does White lose a piece?

Exercise 19: If Black were to challenge the bishop with 2...h6 instead, could White get away with 3 Bh4 or would that ultimately drop a piece?

3 Nc3 Bg7 4 e4

Here is the key the pawn break. Had Black played 3...d5, White has an alternative idea of h2-h4-h5.

4...fxe4 5 Nxe4 d5

Black shifts the central white knight, but now the outpost on e5 is a key square.

King's Indian Defence

1 d4 Nf6 2 c4 g6 3 Nc3 Bg7

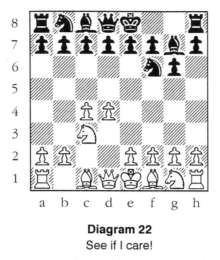

Diagram 22
See if I care!

Here Black has made his mind up on a kingside bishop fianchetto and has happily handed over the centre to White. Although there is no compulsion for White to take up the gauntlet, acceptance of the offer to get in e2-e4 for free is the most thematic continuation.

4 e4 d6

The concept behind the King's Indian is that Black gives up the centre, with the intention of testing White's control of it a little later. However, having said that, Black doesn't want to be overrun and the text prevents 5 e5 (in view of 5...dxe5 6 dxe5 Qxd1+ when the e5-pawn will be a target).

WARNING: Possession of a space advantage is all very well when your opponent is cramped. However, if the odd piece is swapped off and his pieces get 'in around the back', then there is often a good chance of them wreaking havoc.

In many respects this opening resembles the Pirc Defence, but it is interesting to note that there are far more world-class exponents of the King's Indian than the Pirc. I believe the reason for this is that most Black players feel uncomfortable just allowing white pawns on e4 and d4, but feel that if White accepts the responsibility (and tempo lost) of c2-c4 too, then the challenge is really on.

Although occasionally Black may play around the edges with niggly ideas like ...c7-c6, ...a7-a6 and ...b7-b5, usually Black's main decision boils down to whether he will strike at White's centre with ...c7-c5 or ...e7-e5. As usual there are several variations that White can choose from and each branches off into numerous lines of their own. A good cross-section of these is supplied below.

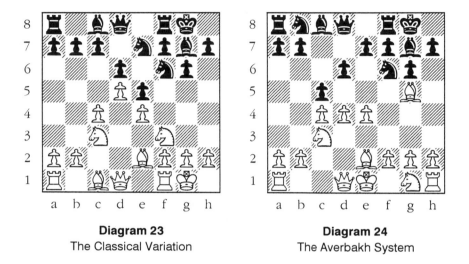

Diagram 23
The Classical Variation

Diagram 24
The Averbakh System

In Diagram 23 we see a variation in which both sides just develop their pieces naturally with 5 Nf3 0-0 6 Be2 e5 7 0-0 Nc6 8 d5 Ne7. More often than not the King's Indian bishop ends up being blocked in by its own e5-pawn in this fashion. However, although it may thus be considered as a comparatively bad piece, the reality is that if it ever escapes, it can often do so to devastating effect. White's pawn chain leads to the queenside and so he will aim for the pawn break c4-c5, whilst Black will move his f6-knight in order to facilitate ...f7-f5.

The Averbakh System with 5 Be2 0-0 6 Bg5 c5 (Diagram 24) is designed to deter Black from playing ...e7-e5. and so he naturally turns to the alternative. White has the option of closing the position with 7 d5, or making the exchange 7 dxc5. In the latter case, 7...dxc5 8 Qxd8 Rxd8 9 e5 could be awkward for Black who instead has the tactical resource 7...Qa5, threatening the e4-pawn and preparing to recapture on c5 with the queen.

TIP: Don't automatically assume that d4xc5 should be met by ...d6xc5. Indeed the temporary sacrifice ...Qa5, avoiding a queen trade, is a common treatment.

Diagram 25
The Sämisch Variation

The Sämisch Variation is a notoriously aggressive system. White bolsters his centre with 5 f3 0-0 6 Be3 Nc6 7 Qd2 a6 8 Nge2 Rb8. Here White can prevent ...b5 with 9 Nc1 and then play positionally with moves like Nb3, Be2 and 0-0. However, it is more fitting to launch a kingside attack with 9 h4. A simple plan is to pry open the h-file for a rook and through Bh6, infiltrate with the queen and thus hopefully (well, not from Black's point of view!) deliver checkmate. No doubt Black will retaliate on the queenside and perhaps throw in ...e7-e5 to give White a reminder that he needs to look after his centre too.

TIP: Usually it is very difficult to organise a successful raid on the enemy king if you have poor control in the centre.

The Four Pawns Attack arises after 5 f4 0-0 6 Nf3. Whilst this set-up looks extremely threatening, Black should not be too intimidated. If White gets in e4-e5, then after the knight retreats he can try and chisel away at White's centre with the likes of ...c7-c5 and ...f7-f6. White must himself be careful not to overreach as although he has a clear space advantage, he has also forgone development whilst advancing pawns and things could easily go wrong for him quite quickly.

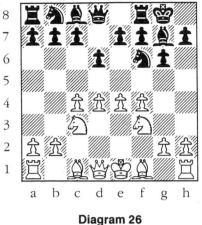

Diagram 26
The Four Pawns Attack

In the above position 6...c5 7 d5 (or as we've seen before 7 dxc5 Qa5!?) 7...e6 will lead to a Modern Benoni-type position once Black trades on d5. And right on cue.....

Modern Benoni

1 d4 Nf6 2 c4 c5

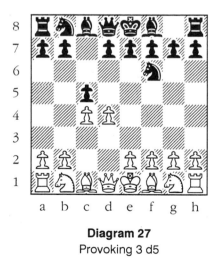

Diagram 27
Provoking 3 d5

Black takes an immediate swipe at the white centre, confident that after 3 dxc5, he would regain this pawn. Indeed both 3...Na6 and 3...Qa5+ would do the trick, whilst 3...e6 is also very sensible. White shouldn't give much thought to that continuation and although he could simply protect d4 with 3 Nf3 or 3 e3, it is more logical to advance the pawn to d5.

3 d5 e6

This pawn break will guarantee a couple of half-open files. Instead, the Czech Benoni keeps things more blocked with 3...e5 (as White won't want to take the e5-pawn en passant any more than he intends to take on e6). After 4 Nc3 d6 5 e4, reaching the position in Diagram 28, Black is very solid, but White enjoys more freedom for his pieces.

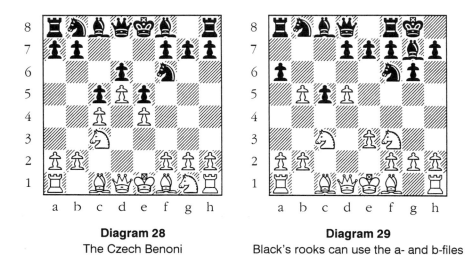

Diagram 28	**Diagram 29**
The Czech Benoni	Black's rooks can use the a- and b-files

Black will strive for ...b7-b5 or ...f7-f5, whilst White's longer-term aims include the pawn breaks b2-b4 and f2-f4.

I also can't let this moment pass without mentioning another club player's favourite, the Benko Gambit. After 3...b5 4 cxb5 a6, Black is obviously prepared to let both his a- and b-pawns go. If the gambit is accepted, it is only one pawn that Black actually loses and he ultimately has compensation through access to two half-open files. Diagram 29 is a typical Benko Gambit position after the moves 5 e3 g6 6 Nc3 Bg7 7 Nf3.

Whilst it's true to say that Black can hold back on ...e7-e6, this is the only way that he will be able to force White to recapture on d5 with the c-pawn. If Black delays with 3...g6 4 Nc3 Bg7 5 e4 d6, which is a kind of King's Indian/Benoni hybrid, one option is 6 h3 (preventing both a future ...Ng4 and ...Bg4 pin) 6...0-0 7 Nf3 e6 8 Bd3 exd5 and 9 exd5 (9 cxd5 isn't bad) when there is no imbalance in the pawn structure and Black has problems finding a home for his c8-bishop.

4 Nc3

White should ignore the idea of effectively trading his d5-pawn for Black's f7-pawn as 4 dxe6 would simply leave Black able to stake a strong claim in the centre with a future ...d7-d5 (as well as allowing him a half-open f-file).

4...exd5 5 cxd5

Exercise 20 Why doesn't White recapture on d5 with the knight instead?

5...d6 6 e4 g6

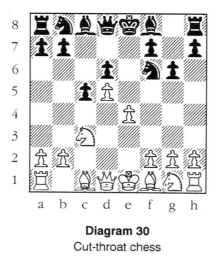

Diagram 30
Cut-throat chess

Here it is fair to say that Black's dark-squared bishop will have a more active role than it does in the King's Indian, as the h8-a1 diagonal will be less congested (compared to the lines where Black plays ...e7-e5). However, White has an extra centre pawn and along with it the chance to steamroll the second player with a future f2-f4 and e4-e5. Black can try and dissuade this plan by utilising the half-open e-file for his own rook, while his queen's knight can control e5 directly (on d7) and a possible f3-knight pin first ...Bg4 could also help him out. We mustn't forget that the imbalanced nature of the position presents Black with an extra c-pawn and White will be eager to prevent his opponent from expanding with the likes of ...b7-b5 and ...c5-c4. It will therefore come as no great surprise that ...a7-a6 will usually be met by a2-a4 and, with both sides working hard to make something of their pawn majorities, a fascinating struggle will result.

Grünfeld Defence

1 d4 Nf6 2 c4 g6 3 Nc3 d5

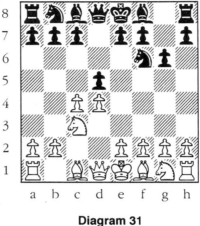

Diagram 31
Leading to an open game

For White after 3 Nc3, the suspense is always there. Will it be a King's Indian (3...Bg7) or will it be a Grünfeld (3...d5)? At first this defence seems very illogical. In the Queen's Gambit, if Black didn't take on c4, then at least he made sure to keep a foothold in the centre (specifically on d5) with ...c7-c6 or ...e7-e6. Here, however, Black appears to casually offer his d-pawn (though not for nothing), thus allowing White a free role in the centre.

4 cxd5 Nxd5 5 e4

Not forced, but certainly the acid test of Black's provocative opening.

5...Nxc3 6 bxc3

It seems as though White has got just what he wants. However, although things seem to have gone his way up to now, the fact is that Black plans to strike back at his opponent's impressive centre and the diagram below will indicate to you the potential for counterattack that Black has:

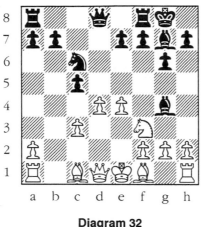

Diagram 32
The d4-pawn is under pressure!

Okay, I have exaggerated the situation by giving Black some extra moves. Nevertheless, it is easy to see how White's centre can quickly come under pressure. This is an ultra-sharp opening and you cannot afford to waste time. Clearly Black can attack d4 with his c-pawn, his queen, his queen's knight and the fianchettoed king's bishop. The icing on the cake is the bishop pinning a knight on g4 and for the latter reason often White opts to develop it on e2 instead (so that f2-f3 would break the pin).

Old Indian Defence

Just like with defences to 1 e4, as well as the main ones, the occasional offbeat openings are seen from time to time, though they are never regularly played by top Grandmasters. I thought I would end this chapter with a couple of these.

1 d4 Nf6 2 c4 d6 3 Nc3 Nbd7 4 e4 e5

In a very similar manner to the Philidor Defence against 1 e4, Black seems happy to keep his distance. Black is content just to bolster his e5-pawn, and there is a possible transposition into a King's Indian variation if he decides to fianchetto his king's bishop. More typically though Black just slots his bishop in on e7 and after castling provides his queen with a home on c7 via ...c7-c6. The latter assumes that White maintains the tension with the likes of 5 Nf3, 6 Be2 and 7 0-0. Of course it would be a matter of taste whether or not he would want to clarify the central situation immediately with 5 d5.

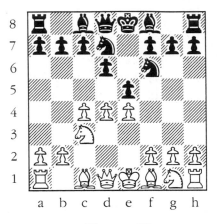

Diagram 33
Non-confrontational!

Budapest Gambit

1 d4 Nf6 2 c4 e5

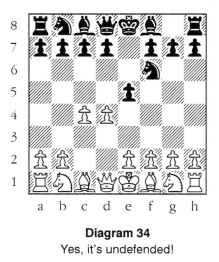

Diagram 34
Yes, it's undefended!

At first glance it may appear that whoever invented this wacky defence (if you can call it that) didn't have his head screwed on properly! Black is apparently sacrificing a centre pawn that when accepted will force him to move his only developed piece a second time.

3 dxe5

3 d5 would be foolish. Black can develop his bishop on c5 before playing ...d7-d6, when there would be some uncomfortable pressure on f2.

TIP: If your instinctive reaction is to advance a pawn when challenged by an enemy foot soldier, be sure to stop and think. Whilst this is often a more than satisfactory response, take some time out to consider exchanging (i.e. just capturing) or in particular maintaining the tension.

3...Ng4

The dubious 3...Ne4 is a genuine gambit that is not to be recommended. After 3...Ng4 White has a variety of ways to continue, but I have selected arguably the main line.

4 Nf3 Bc5 5 e3 Nc6 6 Be2 0-0

All right, I will concede that this probably isn't really a genuine gambit either. For White to play 4 f4 to protect his pawn was far too weakening, and certainly in this safe way that White has chosen, Black can regain the pawn at his leisure.

7 0-0 Re8 8 Nc3 Ngxe5 9 Nxe5 Nxe5

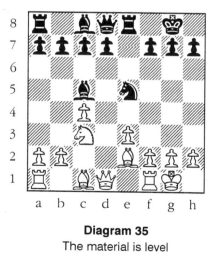

Diagram 35
The material is level

Here it is generally accepted that White has a positional advantage. White has the option of developing his bishop on b2 and, although some crazy attacking ideas such as ...a7-a5, ...Ra6 and over to the kingside have come to light, in particular White's firm grip on d5 makes life very awkward for Black.

Summary

Generally knights prefer blocked positions, with bishops relishing the open board.

When you only have one bishop, try to advance your pawns onto the opposite-coloured squares from your remaining bishop. That way they work in tandem, rather than duplicating coverage of the same squares.

Usually it is very difficult to organise a successful raid on the enemy king if you have poor control in the centre.

If your instinctive reaction is to advance a pawn when challenged by an enemy foot soldier, be sure to stop and think. Whilst this is often a more than satisfactory response, take some time out to consider exchanging (i.e. just capturing) or in particular maintaining the tension.

Chapter Six

Other Openings

- **English Opening**
- **Réti Opening**

Although there are a variety of different ways to start a chess game, it is not really worth dwelling on the likes of 1 b3, 1 b4, 1 Nc3 and 1 g4, against which simple development should suffice. Instead I will round off this book with some brief coverage of 1 c4 and 1 Nf3. Although both are deserving of attention in their own right, it's fair to say that they are closer related to queen's pawn rather than king's pawn openings. Both methods of opening the game usually indicate a quiter start to proceedings than 1 e4 or 1 d4 and both moves are very popular at all levels.

English Opening

1 c4

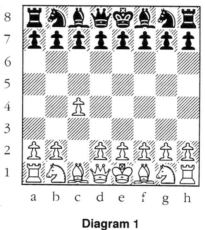

Diagram 1
Not necessarily favoured by Englishmen!

Although no bishops are freed with this move, White immediately exercises control over the d5-square. How Black reacts to this opening should be influenced by his preferred choice of defence to 1 d4.

For example, now 1...e6 2 Nc3 d5 should transpose to a Queen's Gambit Declined (Diagram 2), and if Black is a King's Indian protagonist then the alternative 1...g6 makes sense with developing moves such as ...Bg7, ...Nf6 and ...d7-d6 to follow, though note that the move order 1...Nf6 2 Nc3 g6 is unlikely to transpose to a Grünfeld Defence if White flicks in 3 e4 (Diagram 3).

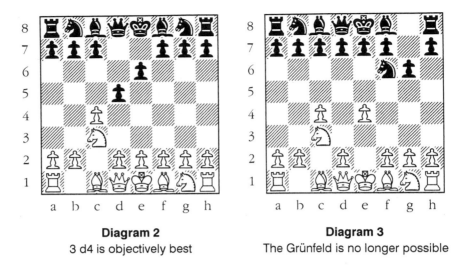

Diagram 2
3 d4 is objectively best

Diagram 3
The Grünfeld is no longer possible

It is easy to be deceived by such tricky move orders and it pays to be on the ball. Here, for example, Black may have been unaware that he would be unable to play his favourite Grünfeld Defence. Sure, d2-d4 will follow, but it is too late for Black to get in ...d7-d5.

A similar problem occurs with Nimzo-Indian players after 1...Nf6 2 Nc3 e6 3 e4 (Diagram 4) as 3...Bb4 would be a case of shutting the barn door after the horse had bolted.

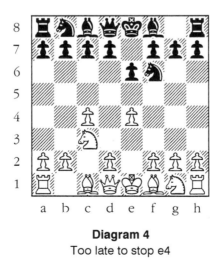

Diagram 4
Too late to stop e4

WARNING: Once you think that you have your openings sorted, beware transpositions into unfamiliar lines.

1...c5

This move introduces the Symmetrical English. The other main reply distinguishing this opening from anything we've seen so far in this book is 1...e5. Usually in this type of reversed Sicilian position White will fianchetto his king's bishop and it is up to Black to decide which formation he wants to adopt. Two popular set-ups are illustrated below:

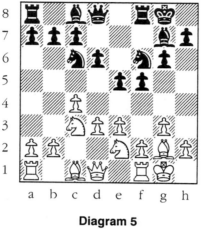

Diagram 5
A reversed Closed Sicilian

This position arises after 2 Nc3 Nc6 3 g3 g6 4 Bg2 Bg7 5 d3 d6 6 e3 f5 7 Nge2 Nf6 8 0-0 0-0 and is basically a reversed Closed Sicilian.

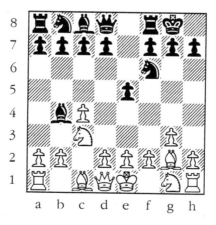

Diagram 6
Black develops naturally

Here we see a logical plan of development for Black with 2 Nc3 Nf6 3 g3 Bb4 4 Bg2 0-0.

2 Nf3 Nf6 3 Nc3 Nc6

This is just a randomly selected variation. The knights could come out in a different order and either side could break rank, not untypically with a kingside fianchetto.

4 d4

Finally the pawn break comes and Black is forced to take as the prospect of d4-d5 is decidedly unattractive.

4...cxd4 5 Nxd4

White has a small space advantage, although it is Black who has the extra centre pawn. Now if Black opts for a fianchetto with 5...g6, then White can construct a useful bind on the d5-square with 6 e4.

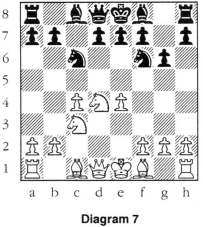

Diagram 7
The Maroczy Bind

Black is certainly not forced into the above though, as 5...e6 is a perfectly acceptable alternative. Also 5...Qb6 (rather early, but nevertheless a safe square) is occasionally seen, the idea being to test out the d4-knight. Note that White will not want to trade knights on c6 as whichever pawn Black recaptures with he will obtain some useful control over the important d5-square.

Réti Opening

1 Nf3

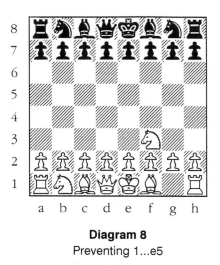

Diagram 8
Preventing 1...e5

Well, there it is, an absolute stunner! Sarcasm apart though, the Réti is renowned for being rather a quiet opening where excitement is at a minimum. As with the English, there are numerous transpositions available to 1 d4 openings, but let's take a look at something that is unique to 1 Nf3.

1...d5

Taking up the challenge, but this is not everyone's cup of tea, since if you are not prepared to play the Queen's Gambit Declined, Queen's Gambit Accepted or a Slav variation, then 2 d4 (with the intention of 3 c4) could be annoying. Instead, 1...Nf6 is sensible and so is 1...c5 provided that you are happy with 2 e4, when you would find yourself playing a Sicilian!

2 c4

Another idea here is 2 g3. Many a Grandmaster has been seen to play 1 Nf3 (or even 1 g3 on occasion) followed by 2 g3, 3 Bg2 and 4 0-0, only then to decide on how they wish to tackle the pawn situation in the centre. One alternative to the c2-c4 break is to somehow arrange e2-e4, as in the so-called King's Indian Attack (Diagram 9).

I'm not entirely sure that playing a Black defence with the

white pieces qualifies it to be an attack, but that certainly seems to be the case here in the reversed King's Indian Defence! In its defence though (or should that be in its attack?!) what often starts off as rather an insipid system often seems to have rather a sting in its tail.

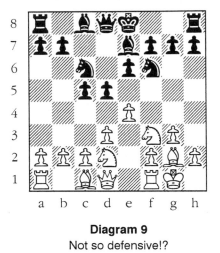

Diagram 9
Not so defensive!?

2...e6

Personally I would be (and indeed have been) tempted by 2...d4. There are always risks involved though, when you try to work a space advantage in the centre with Black, as each pawn move is a move not spent developing and Black is already a tempo down at the start of the game!

3 g3

White also has the possibility of switching to a conventional Queen's Gambit Declined or a Catalan System. Transpositional possibilities are rife in the openings with 1 c4 and 1 Nf3.

3...Nf6 4 Bg2 Be7 5 b3 0-0 6 0-0

The difference between this and a traditional Queen's Gambit variation is that White intends deleting d2-d4 altogether in favour of a queenside fianchetto and a slow build-up which is more likely to include the quiet d2-d3 instead of the more adventurous d2-d4. Black can continue with the obvious space-gaining 6...c5 or perhaps attempt an interesting pawn break plan of 6...a5-a4.

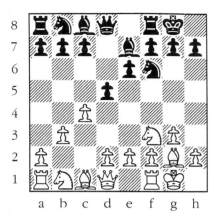

Diagram 10

The b2-f6 diagonal remains unblocked

Summary

1 c4 is similar to queen's pawn openings and will often transpose.

Once you think you have your openings worked out, beware transpositions to lines that are foreign to you.

Chapter Seven

Solutions to Exercises

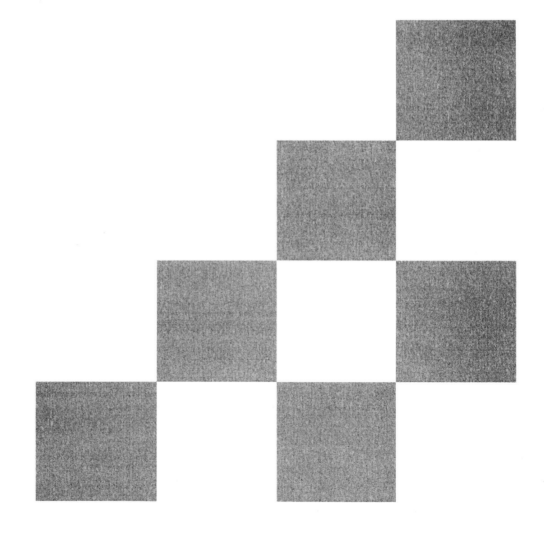

Exercise 1

No. This famous old rule is derived from the logic that generally in the opening a bishop will have more options than a knight. As it makes more sense to make a move that you 'know' you are going to play before one that you are not sure about, it usually follows that you should develop a knight first, waiting to see what your opponent does before committing the bishops.

It is of course pre-determined where a bishop goes in a fianchetto and so once you have decided that that's what you are going to do, there is no need to delay.

Exercise 2

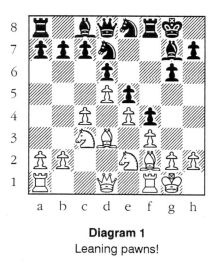

Diagram 1
Leaning pawns!

Okay, so perhaps the wording to this question wasn't great as of course you should always pay attention to what is going on all over the board. However, when pawn chains occur, it is generally true to say that action is best sought in the direction in which the fixed pawns lean.

In the diagram above White's fixed (i.e. blocked by enemy pawns) pawns on f3, e4 and d5 lean toward the queenside. Hence that is the side of the board that he should anticipate making his breakthrough. A pawn break with c4-c5 is the next logical step. If he can achieve that, then his rooks can try and seek entry into the enemy position via the c-file.

In contrast Black's fixed pawns (on d6, e5 and f4) lean toward the kingside and an attack over there with a ...g6-g5-g4 push is a very sensible continuation. The prospects are good for an exciting game.

Exercise 3

Although one general rule tells us not to bring our queen out too early, this is based on the premise that being so valuable, it could be kicked around from pillar to post and is therefore better off staying at home until the coast is clear. Of course it is true that when a more valuable piece is attacked by one of lesser value, then it is obviously not acceptable to just defend it. However, the queen is well placed in the centre of the board (from where it can keep an watchful eye over all proceedings) provided there are no suitable enemy pieces to try and budge it.

In our example, the popular candidate from weaker players is 5...c5, but then after 6 Qd1 leading to the position below, in fact White has come out of things smelling of roses.

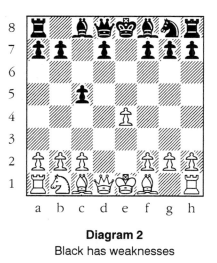

Diagram 2
Black has weaknesses

Although the white queen has ended up where it started, Black has made some irreversible concessions. The d5-square is an outpost (a square protected by a pawn of one's own that can never be attacked by an enemy pawn) which is just begging to be occupied by a white knight. The d5-square will at all times be heavily guarded by White's pieces, so there is little chance that Black's d-pawn will make it there or beyond. Hence it is destined to be a vulnerable backward pawn on d6, where it will receive a battering from White's forces and yet still restrict Black's dark-squared bishop.

Exercise 4

I suppose the answer is yes. However, after 7 Bxf7+ Kxf7 8 Qxd8, Black can win the queen back with 8...Bb4+.

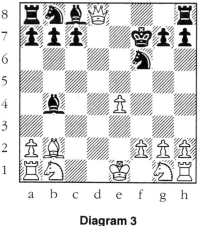

Diagram 3
Watch out for checks!

After 9 Qd2 Bxd2+ 10 Nbxd2, the position is level.

Exercise 5

None of the last few moves have been particularly forced, but on the face of it, in guzzling the offered pawns and boxing his king in, Black does seem to have got himself into trouble.

As it happens these moves were played in a school match I once took part in, when my team's board two pondered this position for some time before resigning. Alas, the obvious saving moves 6...Nh6 7 Bxh6 0-0 suddenly cast a whole new reflection on the position (Diagram 4).

Black is a piece down but has dual threats of 8...gxh6 and 8...cxb2. A close inspection reveals that an attempt by White to deal with both of these fails, i.e. 9 Bc1 Nb4 10 Qd1 c2. Instead White is advised to return the piece with 9 Nxc3. My view is that White's position is preferable, but it's hardly resignable for Black.

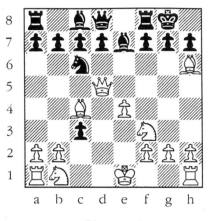

Diagram 4
Still alive!

NOTE: Whilst one should show respect to the opponent, the worst you can do is lose!

Exercise 6

Well, the knights and bishops have been developed and both sides have castled. However, neither player has really given much consideration to how the rooks are going to enter the fray. White might try to liven things up a bit with 8 Be3. Then a bishop trade leading to the position below would leave White with a useful half-open f-file and good attacking prospects.

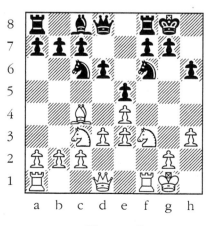

Diagram 5
Both white rooks could use the f-file

That would be a good example of why doubled pawns aren't necessarily a bad thing, but the problem is that Black is far from obliged enter into the swap. He may even wish to encourage a similar deal by placing his own bishop on e6, but if neither side is prepared to play ball, then the stalemate (well obviously not a real stalemate!) will continue.

Exercise 7

I would have to say 'No'! White prevents his opponent from castling, but this can be done 'by hand' and Black will ultimately have a nifty half-open f-file available for his rook. After the obvious 6...d5 leading to the position below, White will also have difficulty with his knights.

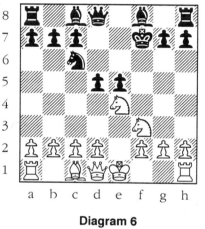

Diagram 6
There is a 'spite' check on g5, but little else

Exercise 8

Well, if you read on, you would have seen that 4...d5 is the only satisfactory method of dealing with this problem. Okay, Black could try to make sure that he doesn't lose the exchange as well as a pawn with 4...Qe7, but that is conceding defeat. For the record though, the crazy 4...Bc5, known as the Wilkes-Barre or Trexler Variation, leads to very complicated play, for example if White plays 5 Nxf7 then he is stunned by 5...Bxf2+ 6 Kxf2 Nxe4+. With ...Qh4 coming, Black generates a wicked counterattack. However, this interesting line is not forced as White can instead bail out with 5 Bxf7+ Ke7 6 Bd5. Theory implies that this simply accepts a safe pawn.

Exercise 9

Okay, this does move one piece twice before moving others once, but after 4 Nxe4 d5 5 Bd3 dxe4 6 Bxe4, things will have worked out fine for Black as he is the one with a pawn left in the centre.

However, the story is somewhat more complicated than that! Instead White can continue with the tricky 4 Qh5. Obviously Black must deal with the mate threat on f7, but he also mustn't forget that his knight remains en prise. The ugly looking 4...Nd6 is forced, when instead of just regaining the pawn with 5 Qxe5+, the cool retreat 5 Bb3 is interesting. With this bishop safe, after 5...Nc6, White can reaffirm his interest in f7 with the decoy 6 Nb5. Ultimately Black is then forced to sacrifice material with 6...g6 7 Qf3 f5 8 Qd5 Qe7 9 Nxc7+ Kd8 10 Nxa8. Although it's a whole rook, the knight in the corner is doomed after 10...b6.

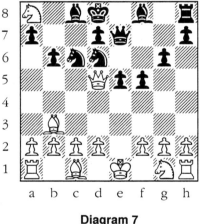

Diagram 7
Adequate compensation?

The white queen looks vulnerable and Black has a nice centre. Whether or not he has enough compensation is a highly debatable point which then gives us the answer that 'Yes' it is possible, but whether it 'works' remains unclear.

Exercise 10

The pin achieves very little here as although 5...d5? 6 d3 would win a piece, 6...Qe7 is satisfactory, e.g. 7 d3 Nf6 when both sides have suffered equally by having their queens prematurely thrust in front of their kings. There would still be play left in the game, but in this type of symmetrical position, White's extra move provides him with only minimal benefit.

Exercise 11

The only good move is to advance the attacked pawn with 3 e5. Alternatives such as 3 d3 are vastly inferior stopgaps and enable Black to take over the centre with the likes of ...e7-e5 and ...d7-d5.

The bonus of 3 e5 is that it forces the black knight to move again and after 3...Nd5, White can continue with his d2-d4 plan. An inevitable trade of pawns with 4...cxd4 5 cxd4 will leave the situation looking like the diagram below.

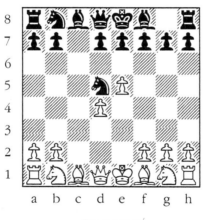

Diagram 8
The d5-square is a potential black outpost

White has an undoubted space advantage with his e5-pawn controlling some useful squares. However, Black has found a nice home for his knight and can try to undermine White's pawn centre with ...d7-d6, ultimately hoping to prove that White has over-extended himself.

Exercise 12

Black must be careful in deciding how to develop his kingside pieces in the absence of the use of the f6-square. The most typical decision is to leave the dark-squared bishop at home until it has something definite to do. The f5-square is a good location for the knight as it helps pressurise the target point on d4. The knight can consider getting there via h6 or e7. Also ...Bd7 will always be useful as it brings this commonly recognised 'bad bishop' a bit nearer the action and vacates the c-file, thus enabling a future ...Rc8 or perhaps ...0-0-0.

Another pawn break that Black can often consider is ...f7-f6, but probably the most popular move here for Black is 5...Qb6. The queen is developed to a safe square where it is surprisingly active. As well as pressurising the d4-pawn, it hits b2, thus significantly restricting the options of White's dark-squared bishop.

Diagram 9
The d4-pawn is a target

Exercise 13

Black wants to play actively and hence we can rule out 4...e6, which makes his light-squared bishop look stupid. One club player's favourite is 4...Bf5. Okay, this is developing a bishop before a knight, but ...e7-e6 must come soon and so it is logical to excavate this bishop first. In dealing with the problem of his attacked knight, White mustn't forget that his d-pawn is also under the beady eye of the black queen. Hence, for example, 5 Bd3? would simply drop a pawn to 5...Qxd4. Theory recommends 5 Ng3 because it forces the enemy bishop to move again, thus levelling up the tempo situation after 5...Bg6.

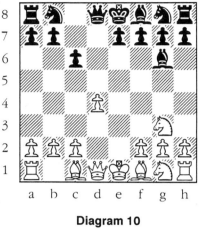

Diagram 10
Is h2-h4-h5 on the agenda?

Here 6 Nf3 is sensible, although White may wish to consider livening things up with h2-h4-h5 sooner or later.

From our original position Black could just develop with 4...Nf6, but it is generally assumed that the structural defects that result from a simple trade with 5 Nxf6+ leave Black very slightly worse off (Diagram 11).

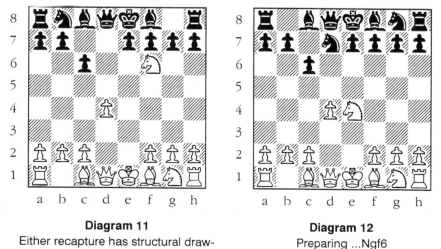

Diagram 11
Either recapture has structural draw-backs

Diagram 12
Preparing ...Ngf6

Hence most Grandmaster exponents of the Caro-Kann these days seem to favour 4...Nd7 (Diagram 12). This prepares 5...Ngf6 such that Black could re-rack this knight if need be, thus avoiding doubled pawns. The likelihood is that White will want to avoid swapping off knights anyhow.

Exercise 14

White has many possibilities and a flashy one is 16 Rxg7+ Kh8 17 Rxh7+ Kxh7 18 Qh5+ Kg8 19 Qg5+ Kh7 20 Qg7 mate.

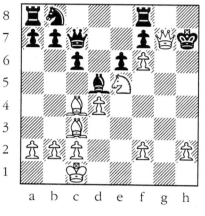

Diagram 13
Impressive!

Exercise 15

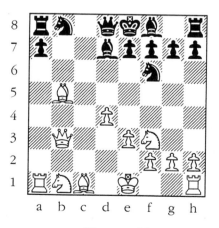

Diagram 14
The a7-pawn is a target and White has an extra centre pawn

The key move to look out for is b2-b3 (either before or after a4xb5 a6xb5). Black can go temporarily two pawns up with 5 b3 cxb3, but White will regain both b-pawns with interest after 6 axb5 cxb5 7 Bxb5+ Bd7 8 Qxb3 (Diagram 14).

Exercise 16

The main tactic is 6 Bxf7+ Kxf7 7 Ne5+ when White regains the bishop on g4, leaving him a pawn up and with the enemy king horribly exposed. White could even try the flashy 6 Ne5.

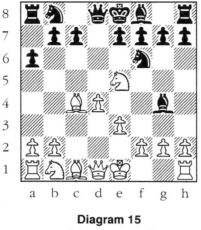

Diagram 15
Take my queen!

Unfortunately, Black's most natural move, 5...e6, prevents all of these threats and White will just have to develop normally.

Exercise 17

I suppose that strictly speaking the answer is 'yes', although after 5 cxd5 exd5 6 Nxd5 Nxd5 7 Bxd8, Black has 7...Bb4+ (Diagram 18).

White's lack of kingside development means that he has to block the check with his queen and this ultimately leaves him a piece for a pawn down.

NOTE: 5 cxd5 (the Exchange Variation) is not a bad move in its own right, but clearly 6 Nxd5 fell into a trap and 6 e3 would have been eminently more sensible.

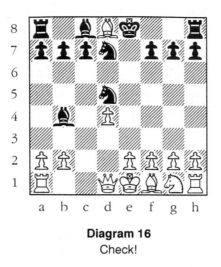

Diagram 16
Check!

Exercise 18

White should really continue with the plan of banishing the knight via 11 f3. Instead 11 g3? opens up the b7-h1 diagonal to his extreme detriment and Black has the dazzling response 11...Ng5! Certainly White doesn't have to take the queen, but if he did, there are worse ways to finish a game than 12 gxh4 Nh3 mate!

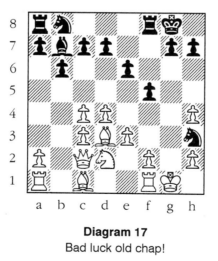

Diagram 17
Bad luck old chap!

Exercise 19

3...g5 is possible, although Black is playing with fire. At the very least White can ensure that he doesn't get his bishop trapped with 4 e3, aiming to meet 4...gxh4 with 5 Qh5 mate.

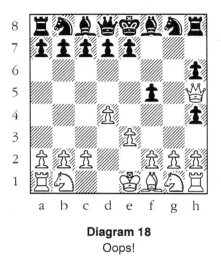

Diagram 18
Oops!

Instead of 4 e3, White can even play 4 Bg3, since 4...f4 fails to 5 e3! with the same idea as before.

Exercise 20

Sure, the d5-square would be an outpost, but of course Black would trade knights. It all stems back to that general principle about avoiding fair swaps when you have a space advantage. In general, White should keep the pieces on in such positions.